The Turkish Republic
at
Seventy-Five Years

The Turkish Republic
at
Seventy-Five Years

Progress – Development – Change

Edited by
David Shankland

The Eothen Press

British Library Cataloguing-in-Publication Data
A catalogue record for this book is available from the British Library

Published 1999

© The Eothen Press, 1999

Published by the Eothen Press, 10 Manor Road, Hemingford Grey, Huntingdon, Cambridgeshire, England, PE18 9BX.

ISBN 0 906719 28 3 (paper)

Printed in Great Britain by Biddles Limited, Guildford and King's Lynn

Contents

Contents

Contributors

Professor Sina Akşin: Political Science Faculty, University of Ankara. Specialist on Kemalism and on Republican History.

Mr David Barchard: Consultant and author. Formerly Ankara correspondent of the Financial Times.

Professor Clement Dodd: Specialist on Turkey and modern Cyprus. Formerly Professorial Fellow in Politics, and Director of the Turkish Studies Programme, SOAS, University of London.

Dr William Hale: Reader in Politics, School of Oriental and African Studies. Specialist on modern Turkey, particularly military and political aspects.

Dr Andrew Mango: Specialist on Turkish affairs. Formerly BBC Head of Service. Biographer of Atatürk.

Mr Akın Öngör: Chief Executive of Garanti Bankası, Turkey.

Sir Michael Quinlan, GCB: Formerly Head of Ditchley Park. Previously, Permanent Under-Secretary at the Ministry of Defence.

Dr David Shankland: Lecturer in Social Anthropology, University of Wales, Lampeter. Formerly Assistant and Acting Director, British Institute of Archaeology at Ankara.

Professor Norman Stone: Head of Department of International Relations, and Director of Russian Studies Centre, University of Bilkent. Formerly, University of Oxford.

Foreword

His Excellency Mr Özdem Sanberk,
Ambassador of the Republic of Turkey to the Court of
St. James

When I decided to hold this seminar, my aim was very simple. This year the Turkish Republic is seventy-five years old. Turkey is an old nation, like Britain. We cherish the memory of our past. But seventy-five years ago we embarked on a new adventure, that of becoming a fully modern country. Now, we are almost at the end of the twentieth century. In this time we have come a long way, but the progress we have made is still perhaps not fully appreciated in Britain. Of course, there is still a gap between Turkey and Europe, but it is now narrower than ever before and it is closing.

Turkey is ending the twentieth century in far better shape than it began. In 1900, Turkey was still economically a very poor and undeveloped agricultural country, with little infrastructure, almost no industry, and with a very high mortality rate. Although, like Britain, Turkey still had an empire, unlike Britain it faced neighbours who were planning to carve the country up and take it off the map. Nevertheless, Kemal Atatürk and the founders of the Republic had a vision of Turkey as a strong, independent, prosperous and modern country, a vision that they were determined to realise from the ruins that they came to inherit.

In 1999 Turkey is a completely different country from that of seventy-five years ago. Its population is perhaps 65 million, five times greater than at the beginning of the century. More than half of those people live in towns and cities. It is overwhelmingly an industrial society. It is the main trading partner of Britain, and the European Union, in the Balkans, Near and Middle East, and southern Mediterranean region. It is increasingly a high-tech society with universities in every large town, internet cafés and satellite television.

It is also a democratic society. It is the only firmly established democracy in the Islamic world and also the only secular state in the Islamic world. By secularism, I mean keeping politics and religion separate, as is the case in Europe. Yet Turkey has not always perhaps been given the credit for this that it deserves. Some people even tell us that we should be more Middle Eastern and more Islamic. This has not proved a successful development route for other countries. Yet I believe that the emergence of a large, strong industrial nation with a pluralist system at the edge of Europe, Asia and the Middle East is an extremely important development for the world system. It is going to be even more important in the next century.

For the seminar, the papers from which are published here, I brought together specialists both from Britain and from Turkey to help us understand the transformation: how it began in the 1920s and 1930s, the part that Kemal Atatürk played, and why he is still revered today in Turkey. Anthropologists, political scientists, historians, bankers, and journalists create a multi-disciplinary approach but one that is not too academic. Through them, I hope that we shall be able to take stock of just how much Turkey has achieved and what still remains to be done after these first seventy-five years of the Republic.

Preface

The papers published here were all, with one exception, given at a one-day conference held to mark the seventy-fifth anniversary of the Turkish Republic. The texts themselves are based on the edited transcriptions of the day's proceedings. Occasionally their respective authors have decided to make slight alterations in order to reflect the difference between spoken and written styles, though the papers remain substantially as given on the day. Mr David Barchard's article is published with the permission of *Cornucopia*, where it appeared in a shorter version.

Whilst celebratory, the conference was also lively, and by no means uncritical. The discussion following each paper was often extremely well informed. Whilst it is impossible to recreate such live enthusiasm, it is hoped that some of this healthy debate comes across here. We have included a selection of the questions and responses after each paper and a substantial extract from the separate discussion session in order to encourage further debate. By virtue of the 'Chatham House' rules under which the day was held, individuals' names are not given.

In preparing this volume, as Mr Sanberk notes in his Foreword, our aim has been to be multi-disciplinary without being too academic. For this reason, technical expressions, and scholarly apparatus have been kept to a minimum. Yet, the varied arguments that are touched upon are of use to the specialist, as well as the general reader in giving little nuggets to think upon further. From among many, one might note Dr

xi

Preface

Mango's point that part of Atatürk's achievement was to create a nationalism that was avowedly non-irredentist, Professor Akşin's stress on 'integrated' development as a founding principle of the Republic that was later partly abandoned, Dr Hale's indication of the popularity of Japan among Islamist groups, and Professor Stone's comparison with the former Soviet Union. Editing these papers has been therefore a pleasant and stimulating task, and it is hoped that they prove to be equally so to the reader.

David Shankland
October 1999

Introduction

Sir Michael Quinlan, GCB

Ambassador, I would like to offer thanks on behalf of us all for bringing us together for this special occasion, and then on behalf of myself for according me the privilege of refereeing the proceedings. Many years of professional work, especially in the NATO environment, have given me a very deep respect and regard for Turkey, so I value the chance to be here.

As you have recalled, Ambassador, the occasion that brings us together is the seventy-fifth anniversary of the establishment of the Republic under the leadership of one of the most remarkable men known to this century or indeed to any other. One can find comparators for one part or another of what Atatürk achieved, but the aggregate almost beggars parallel. Historians debate just how far he was able to develop the seeds sown by others, how far his achievement was one of brilliant opportunism as well as of a clear conceptual vision, and how far he was lucky in the circumstances around him and the mistakes made by his internal and external advisers. But the achievement overall is truly staggering and it was made, moreover, in quite a short time. Last week we marked the sixtieth anniversary of his death at an age which several of us have already outstripped.

Nevertheless, our event today is not just one of celebration, whether of Atatürk himself or of the Republic whose foundation he led. He was an exceptionally clear-sighted and, in policy matters, unsentimental man looking constantly towards the future. I think he would have wanted an occasion like this to be one with a large element of cool stock taking, of realistic recognition of what had not gone well as well as what had, and of facing up to the challenges and difficulties ahead. There are such difficulties as we all know. Elements of the Atatürk legacy are being questioned domestically within Turkey. The external environment around Turkey has been moving at a high pace in complex and sometimes awkward ways. These set new questions, largely different from those which faced the Republic at its foundation, about how Turkey should see herself and how she should fit herself into the changing global scene.

There is a very deep desire here in the United Kingdom, as is the case elsewhere in most of the West, to see Turkey respond successfully to those questions. That desire springs from several sources: from admiration for a remarkable people, from gratitude for the part which Turkey played in the Alliance during the long decades of the Cold War, from human concern for the well-being of some 63 million people and from a prudent awareness in our own self-interest of how crucial a place Turkey occupies now in geo-political terms.

You have assembled, Ambassador, a remarkable array of talent, both in the audience before us, and in the speakers. I now call upon Dr Mango to open the proceedings.

| 1 |

Atatürk's Legacy

Dr Andrew Mango

The Turkish Republic, as it exists today, is the legacy of its founding father, Mustafa Kemal Atatürk. It retains the characteristics with which he endowed it. It is a secular state inhabited by 63 million Muslim Turks. As President Süleyman Demirel put it: 'I am a Muslim. The state has, and can have, no religion, for only individuals can have religious affiliations'. The Republic, again as designed by Atatürk, is a unitary state ruled by a parliament elected on the basis of universal suffrage. The law does not allow any discrimination between citizens on grounds of sex, religion or ethnic origin. Women were given the vote in local elections in 1930, and in parliamentary elections in 1934, when Atatürk was president.

Turkish law is based on continental European law. It has been updated repeatedly in conformity with modern European practice, most recently when Turkey concluded a customs union with the European Union. The constitution guarantees the freedom of the judiciary. Since 1961 Turkey has had a constitutional court, like Germany or the United States, which scrutinises laws passed by parliament. From its inception the Republic has had a Council of State – a supreme administrative tribunal to ensure that the administration keeps within the law. The Republic was designed as a state based on law and it has maintained this character.

Similarly, Atatürk emphasised respect for international law and the observance of international treaties as a principle of his foreign policy. The foreign policy of the Turkish Republic will be discussed in greater detail later. I shall content myself with saying that it has always pursued the objective defined by Atatürk as 'peace at home and peace in the world'. Atatürk wrought a cultural revolution in his country, but he was a believer in law and order. Perhaps his greatest gift to his people was to have inaugurated the longest period of peace that Turkey has ever known.

If today, 63 million Turks lead longer lives and are materially immeasurably better off than the 12 million or so inhabitants of the country in 1923, when the Republic was proclaimed, it is because the country has been at peace. In Turkish history, the empire was synonymous with war, the Republic with peace. Economic progress, achieved in peace, has led to the growth of a large middle class. In Atatürk's days it consisted almost entirely of state employees. Today it is estimated that a fifth of the population – some 12 million people – have an income of more than $10,000 per person. Foreign businessmen are becoming aware of the potential of this large market.

If Atatürk had never existed, a Turkish national state would probably still have been created, although within different, almost certainly narrower, borders. But it might well have been denied internal and external peace. The birth of a new state is usually attended by civil strife, sometimes by civil war. Many examples come to mind – from Greece in 1830 to what was then called the Irish Free State after the First World War. Thanks to Atatürk, the Turkish Republic was spared these troubles. There were isolated riots in the provinces and risings in tribal areas. But the number of victims was small – and that in a country, which had been plagued by banditry for centuries.

Similarly, new states are often tempted to foreign adventure. Again, many examples come to mind – from advanced states like Germany and Italy to Third World countries like Iraq or Libya. Atatürk set his face resolutely against foreign adventures of any kind. From the beginning of the Turkish War of Independence he set out clearly the limits of the territory which he sought for the Turkish national state: it was the land which Ottoman armies still held when the armistice was signed at the end of October 1918 – that and no more. That territory included the province which is now called Hatay and which Turkey regained in 1939. It also included Mosul, which Turkey gave up in 1926. The fate of both territories was settled by negotiation, and it was also by negotiation that Turkey regained military control over the Straits in 1936.

Having secured the territory and the independence of the Turkish national state, Atatürk established good relations with all neighbouring countries. In today's changed circumstances, it is salutary to recall that in 1934 the Greek political leader Eleuphtherios Venizelos, who had originally launched the Greek army into Turkish Anatolia, nominated Atatürk for the Nobel peace prize. Not content with repairing relations with neighbouring countries individually, Atatürk supported collective security – regionally through initiatives like the Balkan Entente and the Saadabad Pact (with Iran, Iraq and Afghanistan) – and globally through the League of Nations, when Turkey took part in sanctions against Mussolini's regime in Italy.

Present-day Turkish foreign policy – its support for NATO and other international organisations, its promotion of the Black Sea Economic Cooperation – is faithful to Atatürk's legacy in a field which is of particular interest to the outside world. Under Atatürk, Turkish diplomacy was extremely active: it remains so today. When he was president it aimed at Turkey's security within an ordered world: it does so today.

This brings to light another aspect of Atatürk's legacy, which is particularly relevant. Atatürk can be described, perhaps paradoxically, as a 'one-world nationalist'. He showed that nationalism need not be a destructive force, that it can promote peace with other nations. There were, among Turkish nationalists, men who wanted to press claims on Mosul and on Greek Western Thrace, which had at that time a Turkish majority; there were men who wanted to retain sovereignty over the Arab Middle East, who hankered after a great Turkish state, which would include Turkic peoples in the Caucasus and beyond the Caspian. Atatürk would have none of it. Rejection of foreign adventure was one reason (the need to preserve law and order at home was another), why Atatürk found it necessary to rule through a single-party regime. The domestic opposition was tempted to outbid the government in patriotism, and competition for power was expressed in a dangerous competition in nationalist rhetoric. Atatürk's advice, 'we must know our limitations', was salutary. He was a rationalist and a realist, and his spirit has shaped Turkish policy to this day.

Atatürk's approach was remarkably balanced. He was acutely aware of his country's backwardness and his people's lack of modern knowledge – what he called 'the cloud of general ignorance' hanging over the country. But he was equally certain that, given the chance, his people were capable of acquiring knowledge. His advice: 'Be proud, confident and hard-working' fostered self-reliance. Atatürk's Republic was established with European inspiration, but without European help. One could go further and say that it was created in spite of Europe. A culture of dependency is contrary to Atatürk's legacy. He employed European experts, including notably refugees from the Nazi regime in Germany, but the Turkish Republic paid for them. Foreign specialists continue to work in Turkey. But Turkey now also exports skilled staff: managers, academics, doctors, and bankers. Atatürk's hope that Turkey would become a contributing member of modern civilisation has been realised.

Atatürk remains both an inspiration and a symbol in Turkey today. True, the symbol is controversial. But this is not surprising. Atatürk's own source of inspiration was the French Revolution and the secular, democratic state to which it gave birth. Loyalty to Atatürk in Turkey today is comparable with loyalty to the ideals of the revolution in France, a sentiment, which to this day, can fill the streets with demonstrators. But there is this difference: the French revolution had many authors and leaders. Atatürk is the embodiment of the Turkish revolution. Thus, loyalty, which flows to abstract ideals in France, is focused on Atatürk's person and memory in Turkey. The attacks by Islamic fundamentalists on Atatürk's memory should not surprise us. Nor are they a sign that Turkey is moving away from Atatürk's legacy. It took France well over a century to accept the revolution as a national achievement. In Turkey, most pious Muslims already accept Atatürk's reforms as a fact of life – for many it is a welcome, liberating fact.

As time goes by, more and more opponents of the secular republic will be reconciled with it. When the leader of the newly formed Islamic Virtue Party recently laid a wreath on Atatürk's grave in Ankara, it may well have been an act of political expediency. It was nonetheless symbolic. The vast amount of space devoted in the media – and, above all in Turkey's own free media – to the current controversies between secularists and Islamists, obscures the fact that Turkey is slowly, but surely, moving towards a synthesis which will be achieved in the framework of Atatürk's secular republic. The more prosperous Turkey becomes, the more closely it is integrated not only with Europe, but with the developed world as a whole, the more quickly this synthesis will come about.

Atatürk's original constituency was the youth of the country which was being trained in new western knowledge. This constituency has grown exponentially. In the days leading up to the seventy-fifth anniversary of the Republic, hundreds of thousands of Turks, young in the main, marched through the streets of Turkish towns, including towns which are usually labelled as conservative, to proclaim their loyalty to Atatürk's ideals. One should consider for a moment what these ideals mean for the present generation. What seems to have moved the demonstrators was, above all, the desire to embrace the modern world.

Perhaps the main characteristic of Atatürk's nationalism was that it was outward-oriented, that it showed the way out of an oriental ghetto. Atatürk was not afraid of the outside world. He had measured himself up against the British, the French, the Russians – not to mention the Greeks and others – in war and diplomacy, and had come out with credit. It was thus on the basis of personal experience that he was convinced that his people were capable of dealing with the outside world on equal terms. Today defenders of the Atatürk legacy share this conviction, while its detractors are people who are afraid of the modern world and want to retreat into a past that never was.

Fear of the outside world, breeding xenophobia, conspiracy theories and, ultimately, an alienation from reality, is far from being an exclusively Turkish phenomenon. It is present in all countries. Its extent in Turkey should not be exaggerated. One of the most striking characteristics of Turkish society today is that most people are ready to go anywhere or do anything to improve their lot. They are open to new ideas; they embrace new technologies with remarkable gusto. In the past, many Westerners used to talk of Oriental lethargy. Now many Turks are surprised to find how laid-back the West can be. What a British correspondent called the other day 'the vibrant dynamism' of Turkish society is the legacy of Atatürk's own dynamism.

Controversy is part of this dynamism. While a few hundred Turkish girls insist on being allowed to wear headscarves in schools and universities, thousands fill discos every night. Islamist publications are widely available, but so, too, are the latest translations of world literature. Films, including art films, are shown in Istanbul at the same time as in London. TV programmes push the boundaries of controversy and of good taste as vigorously as in the West. Turkey is part of global civilisation and culture, as never before. This is the legacy of Atatürk.

Nonetheless, many of my Turkish friends complain of damage to Atatürk's legacy. They instance what they call 'religious reaction', the political stalemate, political scandals. These disorders are the obverse of dynamism and pluralism. But they are disorders all the same. I have already argued that Atatürk was a defender of law and order. He was, in his personal habits, neat and tidy. Above all, he wanted to see a tidy environment. Having spent his childhood in the well-watered countryside of Macedonia, he wanted Ankara, too, to be a green town. He called in foreign city planners to draw up plans for Ankara and Istanbul. The urban and social disorder of Turkey today would have disturbed him. But social change has its own tempo and dynamics.

Atatürk's companion, the journalist, Falih Rıfkı Atay, noted a generation ago that Atatürk's government was strong enough to change the alphabet, but not strong enough to ensure that town plans were respected. But there are signs that society is becoming more alert to the discomforts of disorder. Environmental awareness is increasing. Civil society organisations are springing up everywhere. Turkey is currently in the throes of social, economic, political and environmental restructuring. The process has, admittedly, a long way to go. The developed world could help by embracing Turkey as a partner, sharing the same values.

Not long ago, a prominent Belgian politician argued that Turkey could not become a member of the European Union because Europe was a 'civilisational project'. But Atatürk's project, launched at a time when civilisation was coming under a threat in its European core territory, was a 'civilisation project' above all else. It is this project, which has cultural and spiritual, as well as material components, that forms the core of Atatürk's legacy. And the fact that it is stoutly defended as it continues to be pursued suggests that the legacy of Atatürk is safe sixty years after his death.

Questions from the floor:

Q.   There was one aspect of Atatürk's legacy to which you did not refer and that was the idea and the approach usually called 'étatism'– I wonder if you would say something about that.

A.   I did not mention it because it is what the French would call conjunctural. It was defined at the time of the great depression in 1929 when the entire world was moving towards the New Deal, greater state intervention in the economy and protectionism. It was then Atatürk launched the Étatiste project for the Turkish economy. At the Izmir Economic Congress in 1923 he emphasised free enterprise.
        By 1929 free enterprise could in no way protect the Turkish economy. Turkish exports, which were marginal, collapsed, Turkey could not pay for imports of essential goods, the Turkish currency was shunned. The only way was to move over to protectionism, to a 'clearing' system of barter trade with all its disadvantages. There was no capital in the country with which to industrialise and Turkey received no aid from any country under Atatürk except for one credit from Russia, with which a few textile mills were built. Later, a credit from Russia came also for the construction of a steel mill, which was completed after Atatürk died.
        The situation has now changed. It is true that the state sector, which was built up under Atatürk, is still with us and is a bit of a problem – some would say an albatross because it is much easier to build up a state sector than to dismantle it. But is it a part of his legacy? Some people here may disagree, but I believe the existence of the state sector is conjunctural and marginal. It is not part of the core legacy.

Q.   One could say perhaps that the image of Atatürk has been adopted above all by the Turkish military. Atatürk actually forbade the military people to take part in politics but could one say that one of the 'unfortunate legacies' of Atatürk is that the military and the civilian politicians have often been uneasy bedfellows and remain so today? Is this one of the faults of democracy in Turkey – that the military are still capable of exerting too much pressure on civilian politicians?

A. It may well be the fault of democracy in Turkey but it cannot really be described as part of Atatürk's legacy. It was after all extremely clear that the military were working in the civil machinery of state, and as politicians, the moment they retired from the army, and not before. He did not interfere with the army. He had a head of army, the Chief of General Staff, whom he trusted not to interfere in the running of the civil state. The interference of the army in Turkish politics from 1960 onwards is a result of conditions which came about with the development of market party politics and the tensions they brought to the surface. They cannot conceivably be attributed to Atatürk and his dispensation.

Q. You describe a country which is self confident, coherent and cohesive as Atatürk's legacy. It seems that Turkey today is faced with an incredible challenge in aspiring optimistically, and quite rightly, to membership of the European Union. On the other hand, it is just possible that Turkey could be thwarted in that ambition for some time to come. In those circumstances what do you think Atatürk would see as an alternative role or mission for Turkey as it goes into the twenty-first century?

A. If Turkey were denied membership of the European Union for ever, then it would find itself in the situation that obtained in Atatürk's day, when Turkey was an independent free agent, co-operating *ad hoc* with western powers, in the main, but also with other powers. The idea that if Turkey cannot enter Europe, Turkey will move east or south or in any other direction, should not be entertained. Turkey is not a motor car. Turkey does not move from one geographical spot to another. It stays where it is, pursuing its own interests and its own consistent philosophy.

Turkey will continue to co-operate with Europe within the Customs Union, since Europe accounts for about half of Turkey's foreign trade. Turkey will continue to have the closest cultural ties with Europe since there are many Turkish students here, as there are European academics in Turkey and Turkish academics here. Much of the thought that comes to Turkey comes from Europe as well as from the United States. This organic relationship will develop whatever happens.

Turkey may well one day get rather touchy if more and more refusals come from Brussels and people ask: 'Does that mean that Turkey will give up its European identity?' A European identity is not a document issued by Brussels, which is not valid unless countersigned by Monsieur Santer and Pangaloss, among others A European identity is something which we have, develop, or do not have. Turkey has, to a very large extent, a European identity and is developing it whatever happens in Brussels.

Q.   Could I build a little bit on this last question? Do you see any risk that external behaviour, particularly if it is of an excluding kind towards Turkey, may strengthen internal forces which are hostile to one element or another of the Atatürk legacy, the Islamist, or things of that kind? Might there be a dynamic of that kind?

A.   Yes, but to a very minor extent. It is exaggerated, because a lot of enemies of the Atatürk legacy among Turkish Islamists are people who would much rather go and work in Germany than in Saudi Arabia. One forgets the extent to which Turkish Islamism, like extremism in all countries, is financed by unhappy immigrants. It is a universal phenomenon. One finds Islamic extremists in Birmingham, Macedonian extremists in Canada, and there was the small group of madmen prepared to do a kamikaze attack and crash their plane on Atatürk's mausoleum, who came from Germany, and got their money from Germany. There is an element of psychological discomfort and maladjustment within emigrant communities which leads to support for fundamentalists, for terrorism, extreme nationalism and insane ideologies of all kinds

| 2 |

The Nature of the
Kemalist Revolution

Professor Sina Akşin

Foreigners who visit Turkey are in many cases surprised at the omnipresence of Mustapha Kemal Atatürk. Everywhere they look, they see his depiction in statues, busts, and pictures. I have the impression that they mostly interpret this as a 'personality cult', and tend therefore to think of it in negative terms. This is mistaken. The true interpretation for Atatürk's omnipresence is this: he personifies the Turkish Revolution. This possibility is in itself of interest. Most revolutions are the work of many personalities. The French Revolution cannot be identified with a single person. We do see the preponderance of Lenin in the Soviet Revolution, but he was able to keep power only for seven years after its success, and it cannot be understood without taking Stalin into account. Perhaps the role of Mao-Zedung in the Chinese Revolution is comparable to Atatürk. He ruled China for twenty-seven years. However, his followers well nigh repudiated him.

There is also the question of the relationship between various revolutionary leaders: one cannot help noticing the complementarity of Stalin, Lenin and Marx. With Atatürk, no such complementary figures come to mind. Atatürk is the victorious leader of the struggle for independence, he is the founder of the Turkish Republic, he is the leader of the Turkish Revolution. One can say that he is the complete success story. This is why his person is the symbol of the Republic and its Revolution. Whilst the French Revolution has as its symbol the motto 'liberty-equality-fraternity', Atatürk is himself its symbol. For this reason, you cannot be for the Turkish Revolution and against Atatürk. I think you can, however, be for the French revolution and be against, say, Robespierre, Rousseau, Danton, Voltaire and so on.

For many decades after the death of Atatürk, the great majority of the Turks have felt nothing else than an unadulterated love and admiration for him. It is clear that such a climate of opinion was not at that time conducive to a critical evaluation of Kemalism. Kemalism was explained rather superficially by the official six principles (Republicanism, Populism, Revolutionism, Secularism, Statism, and Nationalism), which were inscribed in the Constitution of 1924. It cannot be said that, in general, these principles were investigated in depth. Criticism and, indeed, hatred, for Atatürk and for all that he stood for existed among Islamic fundamendalists, but until 1945 they were vigorously repressed. They continued to be repressed after 1945, but with much less vigour. Nevertheless, they were generally treated as a sort of lunatic fringe.

Things began to get serious with the founding of the religiously minded National Salvation Party (*MSP*) in 1972, which polled nearly 12 per cent in the elections that followed in 1973. This support for a religious party, and its successor, was to increase over the years. Then, in the next decade, the military junta which engineered the coup in 1980 embarked upon a policy of creating an official ideology called the 'Turkish-Islam synthesis', coupled with a policy of severe repression of the left, including the Kemalists. The curious thing is that all this was done in the name of Kemalism.

With the resumption of multi-party politics in 1983, the left-wing intelligentsia began to criticise the junta. Some of this criticism was also directed towards Kemalism itself. These were the so-called proponents of 'civil society'. Some of them advocated dismantling the Republic founded by Atatürk in order to set up a 'second Republic'. This often violent criticism of Kemalism encouraged many Islamists to come out into the open with negative views of Kemalism. Thus a strange alliance between some of the secular critics of Kemalism and certain Islamists came to be struck. All this was very painful for Kemalists, who were forced to think how the arguments of the anti-Kemalists could be refuted. It can be said that anti-Kemalist criticism has hastened the process of developing a better comprehension of Kemalism. I say 'hastened' because it is natural for a social phenomenon to be better interpreted and understood with the passage of time. Turkey lived Kemalism from 1919 until Kemal's death in 1938, and then again until 1950. Today, Turkey begins to comprehend Kemalism anew, and this comprehension has led to a renaissance of Kemalism.[1]

The Philosophical basis of Kemalism
Philosophically, Kemalism is a movement of the enlightenment. To give a single example, Atatürk indicated this when he called in the name of the Republic for teachers to raise generations with 'free ideas, free consciences, and free knowledge'. Atatürk was adopting the famous formula of the poet Tevfik Fikret, who in a poem had described himself in these terms. Suat Sinanoğlu defines the philosophical aspect of Kemalism as the 'limitless freedom of the mind'. Philosophy professors Bedia Akarsu and Macit Gökberk have also defined Kemalism in this way.

Atatürk was a humanist. His gentlemanly conversation with the Greek Commander, Trikupis, who had fallen prisoner in 1922, his refusal to tread on the Greek flag that was laid out at his feet, and the words he pronounced in 1934 for the Anzac dead all attest to this. On one occasion, he described war, unless fought in defence of the motherland, as a crime. While totalitarian and racist dictatorships were triumphing throughout most of Europe, and many Turks were attracted to these currents, Atatürk stood fast. His invitation and welcome to 142 German academicians thrown out from the universities by the Hitler regime in 1933 because they were Jewish or dissidents, is another eloquent indication in this direction.

Kemalism as a model for development
The Kemalist model of development can be characterised as 'integrated development'. This means wholesale, all-out development. To get hold of the West's machines, instruments, and factories is not enough. Behind this technology lies the West's science. We have to adopt that too. Otherwise the technology we adopt will look and be artificial in our hands. But the upper reaches of science enter into the domain of philosophy. Therefore we have to adopt Western philosophy and the humanities of which it is a part. Naturally we must not forget that social sciences are too part of the sciences. On the other hand, we must not neglect philosophy's relation with the arts and culture in general. Thus, we see that technology, science, philosophy, the arts and culture form a whole.

For them to thrive, we need freedom of thought, respect and admiration for science, culture, the arts and those engaged in these domains. Such persons should not be under the pressure of social, political and religious dogmas. In the Kemalist model of religious development, the creation of a university is as important as the construction of a railway: the opening of a conservatory as important as building a factory.

To understand the model of integrated development, we may contrast it with its opposite, the model of material development. This comes about when a country can afford to buy the latest technology: the most modern cars, aeroplanes, computers, factories but, whilst enjoying the fruits of the latest technology, in respect to social and cultural institutions, lives in the past. In Turkey after 1950, the integrated development model was weakened, and there occurred a shift towards the material development model. Thus, the construction of roads, dams, and factories took first place, whilst social and cultural development was pushed somewhat into the background.

The ideology of Kemalism
The ideology of Kemalism consists of the six principles (or 'arrows') proclaimed by Atatürk's Republican People's Party. The first principle is *Republicanism*. Critics of Kemalism have pointed to the absence of the principle of democracy. To them, Republicanism, with its possible connotations of dictatorial, even totalitarian rule, is not a meaningful principle. This, of course, is a pertinent observation, but it does not quite apply to Atatürk. In 1929, he wrote a school textbook of civics with the aid of Afet İnan. This was published in İnan's name. When she re-published the book in 1969, she disclosed that it was to a large extent co-authored by Atatürk, and included in it photocopies of Atatürk's handwritten manuscript. This included a section on political regimes. According to him, democracy is the best regime, and is superior to constitutional monarchy.

     This commitment to democracy was not just a case of good intentions. While many European countries seemed to be heading towards some kind of totalitarian dictatorship, the Kemalist regime was relatively democratic. A proper assessment of the degree of democracy of a regime can be made by comparing it with other contemporary regimes. Ancient Athens, in spite of so many slaves, foreigners and women who enjoyed no political rights whatsoever, can be called a democracy because it was more democratic than other contemporary regimes. In the same manner, the Kemalist regime, in spite of it consisting of a single party, seems to have provided for more democracy than the average of mainland Europe at that time. It is for this reason that the 142 German academicians who were dismissed from their universities by Hitler's government chose to settle down in Turkey. There is no reason to believe that these academicians, many of whom had brilliant intellects, were so naïve or hopeless as to go from one dictatorship to another. Today, Turkey is more democratic than in the time of Atatürk. However this does not make us happy in itself, because since the post-war period, Europe on the whole, has in this regard overtaken and surpassed Turkey.

The principle of *Nationalism* was of a non-aggressive, non-expansionist, freedom-loving nature. 'Peace at home, peace in the world' was Atatürk's watchword. This nationalism was not racist. Atatürk said, 'Happy is he or she who calls themselves a Turk' (not 'who is a Turk'). The definition of the Turkish nation was 'The people of Turkey who founded the Republic of Turkey' (1929). Every citizen of the Turkish Republic was considered a Turk, whether Greek, Circassian, Kurdish, Armenian, or Jewish. This nationalism was not politically motivated. It did not attempt to impose narrow limits, like making Turkey the most powerful state in the region, or in the Islamic world. It aimed, ideally, at making Turkey competitive compared with all the nations of the world, and in every field - not just in economics, or in military fields, but in art, literature, human rights, and science.

Revolutionism means to spread enlightenment through leadership as widely as possible to everyone in Turkey, to realise integrated development, and to strive actively to achieve these ends. These aims have not yet been attained, and are still relatively far away, but it is necessary to achieve them as soon as possible. Until Turkey has done so, revolutionism should remain on the agenda.

Populism means a policy favouring the people. The concept of 'people' can be (and was) interpreted to mean all classes and groups in the population, but it encompasses primarily low-income groups such as small farmers, workers, and others. It is a policy which tries to promote the material and cultural development of all such groups. It should not be confused with the populism that means flattery of the masses. However, in a multi-party system this is not so easy to resist. In theory, at least, it can be said that in a single-party system policies which are not popular with the masses, but in the longer term will benefit them, are easier to pursue.

The Kemalist regime, except for two attempts at multi-party politics, had until 1945 only one party. If the Revolution has attained an appreciable diffusion among the population, it can presumably continue its development in a multi-party system as well. For it to do so, whilst a single large party may continue to explicitly favour Kemalism, other parties will have also, in the last analysis, to remain Kemalist.

Statism is a principle developed from experience. Turkey's nascent private sector was unable to create an appreciable level of industrialisation in the 1920s. Further, the world depression in 1929 was the cause of much misery. Statism was born of these needs. During the Kemalism era, and afterwards, it was able to create an industrial system. Statism, beyond creating industry and enabling the state to regulate the economy, provided its workers with proper housing, schools, health care, and an appropriate social and cultural environment. In other words, the functions of populism and a welfare state were thereby also fulfilled.

Until 1980, statism performed important functions, not only in Turkey but also in some developed capitalist countries as well. The French automobile manufacturing firm Renault, for instance, has been for many years a successful state enterprise. In the 1980s, a world-wide campaign was launched against the idea of state enterprises. The collapse of the Communist system further enhanced this campaign. Not only in former Communist countries, but also elsewhere, the privatisation of state enterprises has become the order of the day.

As regards Turkey, this can be said. Although the Turkish private sector has made great progress, it has not developed as much as in most industrial societies. Thus, statism will necessarily continue to have a function to perform in Turkey. Further, I do not believe that state management is intrinsically unproductive. In other words, if governments have the political will so to decide, they can make state enterprises profitable. But if they unnecessarily plunge them into debt, if they refuse to make new investments for renovation, if they are filled with workers who are not needed, if qualified managers are not appointed, it means that such governments do not wish state enterprises to thrive. If today the State Monopoly in Turkey can provide the whole country with three different brands of *rakı* (a popular distilled alcoholic drink) but is unable to produce enough beer and matches, this is because it is so desired. The manufacture of beer and matches has been opened to private initiatives. In order that these new private firms may sell as much as possible and thrive, it is necessary that state production should reduce, and that the goods produced by the state be low in quality.

Another point. However much people may be persuaded of the iniquities of public enterprise, they are also aware that they provide employment. Public opinion polls show this. Thus, it is very likely that a party which is more inclined to support privatisation will receive fewer votes. This means that the electors will tend to cast protest votes that will strengthen extremist parties. This is something which is unhealthy for any democracy. As far as Turkey is concerned, at least, until Turkey attains European levels of development, it seems necessary to retain some element of statism. All-out privatisation seems to me to fit very badly with a democratic multi-party system.

Another principle is *secularism*. This is the separation of religion and state affairs. No religion or sect can interfere with affairs of state, and cannot claim any privileges *vis-à-vis* the state. The state's laws and policies cannot be affected by a religion or sect. The state should be impartial towards all religious groups. On the other hand, the state should not interfere with religious affairs. This is the rule, but the state may sometimes be justified in doing so. For example, if a religious group calls its members to practise human sacrifice or wants them to commit suicide, the state should intervene. In the USA, the group called Christian Scientists believe that faith is the cure for illnesses, and they therefore refuse medical care. If a child in that community is suffering from appendicitis and the parents refuse medical care, I think the state should intervene to save the child.

In Turkey, there is an official institution, the 'Directorate of Religious Affairs', that looks after the religious observances of Sunni Muslims. This is an intervention by the state, but I think that it is necessary. It has two advantages. By supervising the majority (the Sunnis), it can prevent anti-secularist movements among them. Secondly, were the Directorate abolished, there would be a great scramble among Sunni groups to control the mosques. In every case, a group (or groups) left out would be forced to construct their own mosques. A large proportion of the national wealth would have to be mobilised to build new mosque buildings. Whereas now, mosques are under the jurisdiction of the directorate and, as such, are open to all.

Some advocates of the *şeriat* system (religious law) perceive secularism as a wrong done against Islam. It is impossible to agree with this view. The *şeriat* was a chain which tied Islam to the Middle Ages. Casting off this chain in Turkey has given Islam the opportunity to become a religion of the modern world. Medieval Islam can have little attraction for modern people. Besides, the abolition of the *şeriat* is for Turkey, and for other Muslim countries as well, a question of development and progress. The *şeriat* calls for the seclusion of women. This means that half the population will be pushed out of the universal race for development and progress. One cannot take part in a race using only one leg. Countries that seclude women can entertain little hope of becoming one of the industrialised countries of the world.

Furthermore, the seclusion of women generally means a regression of their cultural level. Male children learn their tongue from their mothers, not from their fathers. Our most important cultural instrument is our language, and the teaching of language by mothers is the most basic of all education. The basic education of a boy whose mother knows, say, only 500 words will be very different from the basic education given by a mother who knows 1,500 words. Thus, the seclusion of women will negatively affect the quality of the whole population.

Another advantage of secularism is that since it provides for the impartiality of the state before all religious groups, it is a guarantee of domestic peace. In Turkey, traditional enmity between Sunnis and Alevis can be ended only by secular policies. Failing this, we will witness, as we did in 1978 in Kahramanmaraş and in 1995 in Istanbul, bloody fights and massacres.

Some people in Turkey, unfortunately including some statesmen, are of the opinion that 'the state can be secular, a person (for instance a Muslim) cannot be secular'. I disagree with this view. A person who accepts secularism is, for me, a secular person. Such a person can also be a believer (Muslim, Christian etc.). Thanks to the Turkish Revolution, there are many secular Muslims in Turkey, Muslims who accept secularism. Naturally, many of them fully perform their religious duties. As enlightenment spreads, the number of secular Muslims can be expected to increase.

Islam is a religion which has spread to many corners of the globe. It is to be expected that Islam, like all other great religions, should include many branches or sects. They are all Muslim, but they are different from one another. Otherwise, they would not form separate groups. Respect for other groups is necessary for peace and brotherhood in Islam. Secular Islam is now one of these groups, and other sects owe respect to secular Islam, and *vice versa*.

The necessity for the Kemalist Revolution

From time to time one comes across certain observers who seem to assume that the Kemalist Revolution was a sort of personal programme of Atatürk imposed on an unwilling population by a victorious leader. If this were the case, the Revolution would not have survived him for long. It would have soon been dismantled, and Turkey would have gone back to its old ways. However, it is now more than sixty years since his death, and even if the Revolution has been dramatically slowed down since 1950, the edifice of the Revolution is still in many ways intact. Thus, we have to come to the conclusion that the Revolution was an objective necessity, not the whim of a dictator. Let us now see what that necessity was.

The Turks, within the framework of the Ottoman Empire, had achieved the feat of conquering South Eastern Europe up to 'the gates of Vienna'. With the treaty of Carlowitz in 1699 it began a process of pulling back from Central Europe and the Balkans. This withdrawal lasted more than 200 years, the result of successive military defeats. Since Balkan nationalism practised from the very start what has lately been called 'ethnic cleansing', this process has been very painful for the Turks, for very many of whom the Balkans were their homeland. Throughout this ordeal, the Turks had one last consolation: in the last resort, they could live with dignity in Anatolia, whence they had come centuries ago. On the eve of World War 1, the Ottoman Empire still held on to a relatively small piece of territory in Rumelia, namely Eastern Thrace, including Edirne.

World War 1 was another disaster for the Ottomans. However, the peace treaty that the Empire had to sign at Sèvres in 1920 was a traumatic shock of gigantic dimensions for all Turks. They now realised that just as they had been pushed out of Rumelia, now they were being pushed out of Anatolia. The Empire thereby lost not only Eastern Thrace, it was to lose the northern half of the Aegean to Greece, and East Anatolia to Armenia. There was no question of ascertaining the ethnic composition of these territories. These dispositions were purely based on the principle of 'historic rights'. A thousand years earlier there were no Turks in these territories, so the victorious powers had no qualms about parcelling them out, whatever the ethnic composition of the time. The Turks were thus being reduced to some kind of abject subjection in their homeland.

Thanks to the War of Independence, this disaster was averted and the Treaty of Lausanne replaced that of Sèvres. But it became clear that to make the Treaty of Lausanne permanent, the backward social, political, cultural conditions of Turkish society had to undergo radical revolutionary change. That is precisely what the Kemalist Revolution set out to do. If the Revolution had not been launched, it was very likely that the Treaty of Sèvres, or something similar would have reappeared on the first occasion. The aim of the Revolution was to give the Turks as much education and culture as was received by the Europeans, and to make them as productive as Europeans, or in other words, to make Turkey a European country.

The partial counter-revolution

In order to understand better the present position of Kemalism in Turkey, it is also necessary to explain the partial counter-revolution of 1950. Already in the time of Atatürk, counter-revolutionary elements were at work within his party, the Republican People's Party (*CHP*). Probably, no one among Atatürk's followers wanted to go all the way back. The trauma of Sèvres prevented that degree of reaction. What the conservatives wanted was to freeze, or slow down, the Revolution, while preserving the main body of revolutionary achievements. The end of World War II gave them their chance. Turkey's isolation, the result of not participating in the war, pushed İsmet İnönü, successor of Atatürk, into establishing a multi-party system. To make sure that the main opposition party should not question the Kemalist revolution, İnönü partly forced, and partly persuaded, his rivals within the *CHP* to create an opposition party themselves. They did so, calling it the Democrat Party. They were mostly rightist, conservative in orientation.

This rightism was reinforced by two developments. Soviet Russia's repudiation of the 1925 Treaty of Friendship and Non-aggression in 1945, and its attempt to establish control of the Straits and to gain territory in Eastern Anatolia became the pretext for a strongly anti-left, McCarthyist movement. İnönü greatly reinforced this movement by banning socialist parties and socialist publications. This strong swing towards the right also affected the *CHP* itself. Hasan Ali Yücel, the successful Minister of National Education, was one of the foremost architects of the famous Village Institutes and had to abandon his post. His successor set about to downgrade these 'miraculous' Village Institutes. When the Democrat Party came to power in 1950, these tendencies became a general movement. In 1951 the People's Houses (numbering 478), and the People's Rooms (numbering 4322), which were all-round cultural centres, were closed down. In 1954, the Village Institutes shared the same fate.

Gone was the enlightenment programme of the Revolution. The integrated model of development naturally suffered a terrible blow through this development. The Kemalist movement was frozen. To conceal this fact, great emphasis was placed on 'ceremonial Kemalism'. Kemalist anniversaries were commemorated with increasing fervour, and Atatürk's iconography filled every corner of public life. The *CHP* somehow was unable, or unwilling, to conduct an opposition based on the demand for a return to the Kemalist Revolution. Its often very strong opposition was mainly based on a demand for greater political freedom.

After the military intervention or coup of 1960, which brought a new constitution and a great measure of freedom to the political system, intellectuals became attracted by socialism and social democracy, rather than by Kemalism. However, in turn, the fall of communism, the rapid rise of fundamentalism in Turkey, and the heavy criticism of Kemalism gave rise to the renaissance of Kemalism that we see today.

Questions from the floor:

Q.   How might Kemalism be revived in the conditions of modern Turkish democracy? Mustafa Kemal was a democrat but he had a conception of democracy which stressed public interest, and specifically that members of parliament should look after the public interest.

In most modern democracies, and specifically in the Turkish one, there is a great concentration on private interest. There are members of parliament, who are concerned with their own interests and their constituents' interests. There are business groups looking for their own interests and political groups prepared to use the machinery of democracy in order to overthrow it. The only institution that has been able to intervene and stop this so far is the military.

A democracy works ideally through a balance between public interests and private interests. At the moment in Turkey, this balance has not been obtained. Do you see any way in which these Kemalist principles regarding democracy can be restored to modern Turkey?

A.   The military are part of the political scene of course. In recent times, this has been illustrated afresh in the recommendations of 28 February 1997, when they forced the civil government to adopt eight years' obligatory education. It is of course a great discredit to the political parties that the military had to intervene to take this step. Actually a law had been passed in 1973, whereby eight-year education would be compulsory, but there was a provisional article which permitted it to stay as five years. It stayed that way for nearly a quarter of a century. This lack of interest of the political parties means that the military are now in the game.

It is worth looking at this historically. The Committee of Union and Progress did not set up its own governments in the first years of the second constitutional period. From 1908 to 1913 it played a role from a distance. It was giving directives to the government, which were applied or not applied. It seems that this game of government from afar is continuing.

Q.   Is Kemalism a living heritage for students today, and if so, what does it mean and why do they adopt it? Do they regard it as, say, bible teaching is regarded in this country?

A.   The revival of Kemalism is easy in one respect because it is so widely accepted, but it needs to be understood also in the context of what might be termed 'ceremonial Atatürkism', in which people who are not really sincere may take part. For this reason, everyone claims to be a Kemalist, even the Welfare Party say that if Atatürk were alive, he would be a member of their party. In spite of this, very many people do feel very genuinely passionate about Atatürk's ideas. There is a large organisation, the 'Association for Atatürkist Thought', which has nearly 390 branches now, and is nearing 100,000 members which illustrates this.

| 3 |

The Turkish Economy Today

Mr Akın Öngör

My aim in this paper is to offer a summary statistical overview of the rapid and varied progress that has been made by the Turkish economy in the twentieth century. These statistics make remarkable reading indeed. We may recall that, in the late Ottoman years, Turkey's total GNP was only $400 million, and *per capita* income was $40 per person. The country was mainly agricultural and the economy was managed by France, Germany and Belgium. The empire was worn out because of the ongoing wars. At its end, as Dr Shankland stresses in his paper on social change, the population was only 12 million and more than 80 per cent lived in rural areas.

Overview
In the first years of the Turkish Republic, that is, between 1923 and 1929, Turkey's GNP was $572 million, and the *per capita* income was $47. The agricultural share in the total product was high, about 45 per cent. Export products were mainly agricultural: raisins, tobacco, nuts and such like. All industrial goods were imported, including basic textiles. The volume of exports was $82 million and the volume of imports was $112 million. There was an annual $70 million deficit in the balance

of payments. About $150 million of foreign debt was inherited from the Ottoman Empire. There were twenty-two national banks most of which no longer exist. There were thirteen foreign banks including the Ottoman Bank, which became part of *Garanti Bankası* two years ago. This was the central bank of the Republic and it printed the currency in those years. The population was still low, about 13-14 million. Literacy did not exceed 10 per cent. Life expectancy at birth was a mere 44 years, infant mortality was very high: 235 per 1000. There was no health service. There were about 13,000 people per doctor ('doctor' included dentists also). There were only nine universities, telecommunications were rudimentary, and the electricity infrastructure in very poor condition.

In contrast, Turkey's GNP today is $204 billion. Even this $204 billion is not a representative figure because Turkey has a large unrecorded economy. According to the state planning organisation and international organisations, after purchasing power parity is taken into account, the GNP is nearly $370 billion, which makes Turkey one of the 17 biggest nations in the world economy. Thus, in only seventy-five years, national income per capita has increased from $47 to $3,200 in the recorded economy. When the unrecorded economy is taken into account, the figure is close to $5,500 per capita.

This enormous increase has been achieved through consistently high average growth. Throughout the first few years of the Republic, economic growth averaged 5 per cent. Although there have been blips, as during the Second World War years, this expansion has been maintained, and has even accelerated in more recent decades. At the same time, there has been a major restructuring of the economy: not just agriculture but now industry and services make large contributions. Today, the share of industry is now 25 per cent of total production.

Foreign Trade

This structural change can also be seen in foreign trade, which has reached $77 billion, up from a mere $138 million when measuring began. Throughout the 1970s exports were very low (only about $500 million in the late 1960s). Today they have reached $29 billion. Agriculture now constitutes only 9 per cent of Turkish exports; industrial exports include computer monitors, textiles, ready-made garments – it seems anything, to any country. As for imports, the main products are raw materials and investment goods with consumer goods constituting only 14-15 per cent of the total. Tourism has also become a very important industry for Turkey. In the late 1960s one might have bumped into a couple of Germans in Antalya, for example, but now Turkey hosts 10 million tourists each year. Compare this figure, for instance, with that for Brazil, which is very popular, but has only 2.5 million tourists per year. The contribution of tourists to the Turkish economy is about $9 billion.

Turkey is also now a producer of cars: Fiat, Hyundai, Toyota, Honda, Mercedes and Renault. Indicators show that annual automotive industry production has reached 450,000, up from 1,100 in 1970. The production of electricity is now approaching 5,000 gigawatts compared with only 45 in the beginning years of the Republic. Ground transportation has improved with the construction of roads. There has been a great leap forward for Turkey in annual cement production, which increased tremendously from 268,000 tonnes to 38 million tonnes after the 1980s. Annual textile production from 1960 onwards increased to about 1.5 million kilometres of textiles yearly. The population per physician has dropped to 859 people per doctor. This shows a tremendous growth in the quality of life. The ratio of insured people is about 84 per cent compared to zero at the beginning of the Republic.

The current account deficit now lies at 1.5 per cent of GNP. The end of year figure for 1999 is estimated to be around 1.7 per cent – a manageable figure. This does not take into account the unrecorded shuttle trade which Turkey enjoys with the former Soviet countries. Turkey is very dependent on capital inflows: savings in the country are not sufficient to continue to satisfy its needs. When one relates capital inflows and growth, it is clear that the more capital inflow Turkey receives, the higher the growth rate. In spite of this need, Turkey has not been able to attract foreign direct investment like the Indonesians, for instance. Among the reasons for this are the inflationary environment, political instability, and huge public sector deficits, which have resulted in more inflation and volatility in the markets. Even here, though, there has been an improvement in the 1990s. The foreign debt ratio has dropped to about 25-27 per cent and in 1998 to 24 per cent. It should also be noted though, that having lower foreign investments turned out to be an advantage for Turkey in the wake of the present global financial crisis, as Turkey has not been as affected as have Brazil or the Far Eastern countries.

The public sector
Turkey's deficiencies lie mainly in public finance. The quality of politicians is a perennial source of complaint. Politicians clearly have not been able to manage the country in the way that they should. The large public sector debt has come about because of subsidies for the agricultural sector, deficits in the social security system (which is very badly managed), the loss made by state enterprises, whose purpose is more political than economic, and a huge domestic interest burden. Figures for the consolidated budget deficit show that this burden is increasing.

In response to this, and in common with many countries, privatisation has been increasingly seen as the way to combat public sector inefficiency, and privatisation revenues increased a great deal in 1998. The government today has performed better than other recent governments in this area. They have achieved receipts of about $2.2 billion and they will probably achieve $6 billion by the end of 1999, with the electricity distribution network, GSM licence, and the others in the pipeline. Privatisation is definitely the appropriate way to develop: if not privatised, political instruments disturb the economy very badly.

Banking
Turkish banking assets amount to 50 per cent of the GNP, 30 per cent, if the unrecorded figures are included. In developed countries bank assets consist of perhaps five to six times the GNP, so these assets are small in Turkey, and there is large potential for growth. The share of state banks is diminishing continuously, and private banks are taking the lead. Total state banking assets are 39 per cent, and the remaining 61 per cent private. The state banks remain mainly instruments for politicians. They must be privatised in the future if corruption, and the use of banks in non-economic ways is to be stopped.

Human resources
One of the main strengths of Turkey lies in its human resources, both men and women. Turkish family structure is far more matriarchal than is often realised, and women play an equally significant role in the economy. In the *Garanti Bankası* there are 4,500 employees. Of these, 51 per cent are women. In middle management 40 per cent are women. In senior management 30 per cent are women. This is something one would not find in London. As yet, unfortunately, this is not reflected in parliament but it is hoped that women will take their part in the decades to come.

Comparisons
Comparing Turkey with other emerging markets, for example, with Brazil, Argentina, Poland, Philippines, and Hungary, helps to make clear just how much progress Turkey has made. One factor that emerges is that the current account deficit to GNP ratio is better than in these other emerging markets. Growth too, is healthy, in the last 16 years Turkey's economic expansion has been 4.2 per cent compared with that of Latin

America at 3.3 per cent. World Bank indicators show that Turkey, because of its annual growth of 5 per cent, is one of the fastest integrators into the world economy. The ratio of foreign trade to GNP has risen from 23 to 35 per cent, and the share of industrial goods has also increased.

In addition, in recent years, Turkish private companies have begun to receive quality awards from the European Fund of Quality Management (EFQM).

Turkey, with aches and pains, has come a long way and has got a great future ahead, possibly with a great deal more pain, but there are also, as these statistics indicate, many reasons to be optimistic.

Questions from the floor:

Q.   Could you consider the way in which proxy measures, such as cement production or energy consumption can get us a bit closer to understanding the size and perhaps even the character of the unrecorded economy?

A.   The unrecorded economy consists mainly of tax evasion. It does not derive from smuggling or narcotics or anything of that kind. For example, textiles may be produced, but the manufacturers may not make out invoices: in this way they do not pay taxes. We have a map in our bank. In certain towns, if the balance sheet shows assets of 100, we know that the volume is close to 600 or 700. Our bank has the indicators, the statistical background. Since we are not the tax office we are able to make calculations in this way. We do not judge the customers *per se* on their finances, which is very easy in England, Switzerland or in Germany. Rather, we visit the customers and see what the volumes of business and the flow of funds in and out are. A good indicator of this sort of unrecorded economy is electricity consumption.

Unemployment in Turkey is overstated all the time because the unrecorded side is not recorded in employment either. If one tries to find somebody to build one's garden wall, it is almost impossible to find people out there to do it, yet most of them are not recorded as employed. So Turkey has a large unrecorded economy. There has been an interesting attempt by the Tax Office, very rightly, to introduce a new tax system to encourage people and to include them under the taxed or recorded economy, but it will take some time to accustom people to this change.

Q.   You have given a very healthy picture. In this connection, I would like to ask about the European Union and Turkey. Britain, prior to its entry into the European Union, found it useful to use people in the banking profession as well as in parliament to assist with preparatory work. Could you tell us whether, in fact, the *Garanti Bankası* is being brought in to help the government with Brussels in order to see what might be done in getting this sort of picture across? This is such an important exercise.

A.   The bank has been consulted by officials, not only on the European Union, but also on the economic front as how to curb inflation. There is a fantastic group of bureaucrats in our country. The quality of the bureaucrats is very impressive, in both their experience and in the work they do. The quality of politicians, who manage the country very badly, is very low. That is why we have high inflation. But we have been consulted in general on those issues. The banking sector is international. In whichever country one does business one develops connections with the rest of the world, with the euro, with the European Union, with many projects all over the world. Incidentally, the Turkish banking sector has also prepared itself electronically, systematically, for the year 2000.
    The European Union matters. Everybody supports the idea of Turkey's joining, but the general opinion is that Turkey will not be a member of the European Union within the next decade. Nevertheless, the bank gives its consultations to the

government when asked, though mainly to bureaucrats. Dialogue with bureaucrats is better in general because bankers are not always on the same wavelength as politicians.

Q.   Could you tell us more about the spatial dimension of this economic growth? It seems there has been a fantastic growth in medium-sized towns in Turkey, namely Kayseri, Denizlik, Gaziantep, Çorum, so that growth is moving from the main metropolitan areas towards rather small but mainly indigenous type of growth based largely on the manufacturing sector.

A.   Turkish growth started with the establishment of the Republic and was mainly generated through 'étatism', through the state. There was no capital, there was nothing, so Atatürk started with étatism, which was right. It was the state which took the initiative in opening factories, developing industry and educating the people. After the 1960s the private sector began to take more of a role and in the 1980s, and even more so in the 1990s, the private sector took the lead. In recent years the development of medium-sized companies has led to their assuming the locomotive function in economic growth rather than the large conglomerates: consequently they have dominated the Turkish economy. Istanbul, and other cities in Anatolia, where these medium sized companies are located, are booming and it is very healthy for the development of the country. In our bank we adopt strategies in line with these developments.

Q.   The present British government has set great store by stability and low inflation, which the Prime Minster describes as 'sexy'. Are you not somewhat complacent about inflation in Turkey? It is constantly held up as one of the horrors of modern life, that inflation can destroy all these dreams.

A.   There is a very good model which really asks all the economists to rewrite the theories, that is, the experience of the United States. They, right now, have high trade and low inflation. In the case of Turkey it is therefore believed that inflation can go down to a bare minimum. This can be done, not easily, but it can be done. There is a consensus that if it is brought down, redistribution of wealth and income disparities, among many other things, should be much better. Life in general would be much easier. The main reason that inflation remains high is the populist approach of successive governments. This is why I always criticise the politicians. They promise that they will decrease inflation but when they come to power, they give high subsidies to tea, tobacco, products which they burn afterwards because of excess production. It is common knowledge as to how this inflation can be brought down. As bankers in the private sector, we complain about this and we produce our inflation adjustments, which is a big complication, but which shows the real world. It is true to say too that there is more and more public pressure on the politicians that inflation should come down. We think that the existing government has done a better job than previous governments, although they are a minority in a coalition government, which has made it difficult for them. They have done a better job than we thought they could do. They have started to decrease inflation from 100% to 60% or 70% and it will probably be 40% or 50% next year. The OECD estimate for the year 2000 is about 20% or 25%, which is very optimistic.

Q.   In recent years we have been hearing more and more about the so-called Turkish Mafia and also links between the politicians and the Mafia. What would you say is the impact of this so-called Mafia on the Turkish economy?

A.   In this context, I think there is one word which is good–cleansing. Unfortunately, there is a weak link in the

Turkish economy. Ethical values are lacking. We are strong believers in our company that ethics must be a non-negotiable value. However, when one is ethical one loses business. Even though we lose business, we still stand for being ethical. The fact that the connections between politicians and the Mafia have become clear is potentially good for the country: it is a chance to open up, to clean the relationships and bring in front of public opinion the consciousness that such relationships exist and should be penalised and stopped. This is a very good move. At the moment, this problem is quite rightly highly criticised by universities such as Harvard, but when properly cleansed, Turkey will lose its position in international corruption statistics' tables, and will move from the upper levels to the very low levels. In the coming years I believe therefore that these scandals will lead to a more ethical approach to politics.

| 4 |

The Changing Urban and Human Landscape

Mr David Barchard

If a Martian time-traveller was parachuted into Britain or France in the early 1920s and then again at intervals until the 1990s, he would probably be more impressed by the continuities and survivals than by the changes. Indeed one suspects that many of the changes, particularly the buildings of post-war Britain, would dismay and annoy him. He would be reassured by what persisted: the Eiffel Tower, Belgravia, Oxford and Cambridge Colleges.

But if you took the same alien time traveller and let him travel through the three quarters of a century of the Turkish Republic, he would come away with a completely different set of impressions. A shattered and backward land, which in some respects had not advanced beyond where it was in antiquity would have become a modern industrial state with a relatively prosperous and well-educated population living in the age of satellite TV and the Internet. The Turkish Republic would strike him as a classic case of successful modernisation. As such it should give hope to other countries with developing economies. It also deserves to be much better understood by opinionated commentators in the British press whose knowledge of Turkey is inversely proportional to their readiness to tell the Turks how to conduct their affairs.

Other papers in this volume consider this transformation in its economic and sociological aspects. My aim in this chapter is something much simpler. It is to describe and portray the changes of the last 75 years, many of which may not even be immediately obvious to non-specialists.

What follows is an attempt to envisage a bird's eye view of the Turkish scene, taken from the centre of Ankara, during the life of the Republic. Ankara itself, it may be worth adding, is one of the principal achievements of the Republic. Seventy-five years ago a small provincial administrative centre of around 29,000 people, it has now become a thriving metropolis of around 3.5 million. Without Ankara, regional inequalities and the westward skew of Turkey's resources to the Marmara-Aegean regions would be very much stronger. Istanbul itself would be a city of gargantuan proportions. It is already Europe's largest city with 12 million people. If Ankara had not been made the capital, Istanbul would probably have passed the 20 million mark by now. This is a classic example of a successful 'second city' strategy being employed in urban development.

What follows is an unashamedly descriptive attempt to present an overall summary of the changes which Turkey owes to the Republic and the vision and energy of its founders, qualities which, as we shall see, have been persistently underestimated by many observers throughout the last eight decades.

29 October 1923
In the autumn, when the Turkish Republic is proclaimed, Ankara is a town of some 29,000 people. Few towns look less like a potential capital of a large country. A few provincial

office buildings and hotels are clustered around the square, which today we know as Ulus. Keçioren and Gaziosmanpaşa are outlying summer resorts. Çankaya is just a villa on a hill. The War of Independence has been mostly directed from the buildings inside the Citadel, which as a result have been preserved to this day as a memorial to the national struggle.

This Turkey is a country of around 13 million people. It has lost about 5 million people to famine, disease, and eleven years of continuous war. The Arab provinces of the former Ottoman Empire have broken away and, after the defeat of the invading Greeks, modern Turkey's frontier and identity have been recognised at the Treaty of Lausanne.

Istanbul has just returned to Turkish rule after nearly four years of British occupation. The proclamation of the Republic leaves the last member of the Ottoman dynasty in Istanbul with the religious office of caliph. He is Abdulmecit, among other things an accomplished oil painter. Western diplomats are not sure what to make of Mustafa Kemal, the nationalist leader in Ankara. 'Innumerable projects are discussed [at Angora] and few definite decisions appear to be taken.' writes Nevile Henderson, the British Chargé d'Affaires in Istanbul. Displaying the political acumen which will eventually make him Neville Chamberlain's choice for ambassador to Germany between 1937 and 1939, Henderson describes Mustafa Kemal, the first president of the Republic, as a 'tired hero'.

In fact the new regime in Ankara is about to embark on a massive programme of constitutional, legal, and social reforms intended to be the building blocks of a total new nation. Over the next two years, legislation for a national secular education is enacted (March 1923), religious courts and religious laws are abolished. The number of clergy is reduced by decree. The wearing of the fez is forbidden by law. Dervish convents and shrines are shut down and the international calendar is adopted.

Behind all these changes is the Nationalists' realisation that the new Turkey, in which there are only five cities of more than 100,000 people and 52 communities with over 10,000, has to move fast. National sovereignty assured, the emphasis of the new government switches to accelerating social and economic development to turn an underpopulated agrarian country into a modern industrial nation. The emphasis on economic development remains one of the key goals of Turkish nationalism in the decades ahead, a fact which is consistently underestimated by foreign observers.

Two former army officers, both still around forty, head the drive towards change. Both Mustafa Kemal Atatürk, the President of the newly proclaimed Republic, and his main lieutenant, İsmet İnönü (who became prime minister on 29 October 1923) are career officers who have enhanced the reputations they made during World War – one by leading the Nationalist armies against the Greeks. Together, they will set up a single party parliamentary regime to create the new Turkey. The odds against their succeeding seem high. As a result of the departure of the Christian minorities of the Ottoman Empire, Turkey has almost no industrialists, nor a commercial class outside Istanbul. Even craftsmen and artisans are in very short supply. Getting things mended is often almost impossible.

But the arrival of the Republic means the return of peace to Anatolia. Though the new Turkey has little capital, it no longer has to finance the burden of a large empire, and it has a relatively sound administrative structure. About four fifths of the Ottoman civil service and officer corps have been inherited by the new state.

And there is music. In Istanbul, the twenties have already arrived. Seyyan Hanım is singing tangos, the first western-style pop music in Turkey.

The leadership of the early Republic proved much more durable than that of any other east European state. Turkey's revolutionary ideology struck root. A social class grew up which was strongly committed to it, and its emphasis on continuing economic and social transformation within a secular context. Economic growth turned out to be slower to achieve than institutional development, and was affected by changes outside Turkey, particularly the great depression.

With World War Two, Turkey again faced an urgent challenge to its independence. It surmounted this successfully by remaining neutral during the war. When peace returned, Turkish leaders rapidly realised that the Soviet Union and the United States would now dominate the international scene. British support for Turkey, important until 1947, faded as it became clear that Britain no longer had the economic strength needed for a superpower role. Britain had been Turkey's main trading and political partner through most of World War Two, despite Turkish neutrality. After the war ended, the United States took Britain's place but partnership with it meant a strong commitment to multi-party politics and free elections across the world, and to free enterprise in business.

Turkey in the 1930s had been based on the twin principles of a single party political system and a closed economy. A major change of course was now necessary. Perhaps it was not as great a change as it seemed. Atatürk was a liberal in both politics and economics. He had always believed in free enterprise in economics and parliamentary democracy as goals for the Republic even if conditions dictated different approaches during his own lifetime. It was left to his lieutenant and successor, İsmet İnönü, to launch Turkey upon a new course.

October 1948
Twenty five years on, İsmet İnönü is into his tenth year as President of the Republic after succeeding Atatürk on his death in 1938. Turkey's population is now 19 million. Three quarters of the people still live on the land relying on subsistence agriculture. There are only 1,700 tractors in the country. But there are now 15,000 village schools (for 40,000 villages) compared to 6,000 ten years earlier.

Ankara has turned into a sleek town, with a wide boulevard, stretching for eight kilometres from Ulus to

Çankaya, where the presidential palace is based. It has a population of 150,000, which everyone considers to be very rapid growth.

Atatürk, the founder of the Turkish Republic, has been dead for almost exactly ten years. His body lies in state in the ethnographical museum building while Anıt Kabır is being built at the outlying hill of Rasattepe, the modern Anıttepe. But his spirit continues to inspire people and his Republican People's Party is still in power.

İnönü, Atatürk's deputy ever since the War of Independence, is now the second president of the Republic. As prime minister and president, he has encouraged statist reform policies inside a single party framework. But he is also a convinced democrat and since becoming president, has been pushing steadily for the eventual liberalisation of the political regime along multi-party lines.

By keeping Turkey neutral during World War Two, he has shielded it from the armies of Nazi Germany and Soviet Russia. But the rise of the United States as the dominant world power, and the Soviet threat, is forcing changes in Turkey's policies at home and abroad. The Russians have refused to renew their 1924 Treaty of Friendship and Neutrality, and demand control of the Straits as well as Kars and Ardahan.

Turkey's first application for Marshall Aid is rejected, but eventually accepted. For two years, there has been a powerful opposition grouping in the Grand National Assembly. This is the Democrat Party headed by Celal Bayar and Adnan Menderes. It is clear that the next general elections will have to be free. As a result public opinion now has to be factored much more strongly into policy-making. One sign of this is that religious education is being reintroduced into primary schools on an optional basis. Sir Peter Kelly, the British Ambassador, records in his memoirs that some deputies in the Assembly tell him that they think some religious education might be a good thing.

Ankara now looks very different from the small provincial centre of 1923. It has blossomed into a small eastern European-style city of 225,000. It has wide and spacious boulevards, and chalet-like houses with gardens. In winter, sportsmen go ski-ing on the slopes of Yıldız behind Çankaya.

However on the slopes of Altındağ, opposite Ankara castle, the first immigrants from the country side are beginning to settle. Their houses are the forerunners of the *gecekondu* (shanty town) areas which at their peak in the early 1980s will be the homes of two out of every three of the metropolis' inhabitants.

Turkey now has fledgling industries, mostly set up in the 1930s and almost all belonging to the state. They make staple industrial goods for the domestic market. Though state employees live fairly well, times are tough for people in the villages who are about to be given the right to decide the country's future.

One effect of İnönü's presidency is that western classical music and the ballet have struck new roots in Turkish society, with conservatories being opened in Ankara and Istanbul to train young artists.

For many years, Turkey's experiment with multiparty democracy was both unusual and difficult. In the early 1970s, none of Turkey's neighbours was a democracy and when foreign commentators tried to find a parallel to Turkey, the nearest example was often Indian democracy. Liberalisation of the political system released a good deal of protest. Middle Class radicalism became a factor in national life for the first time. The annual average of economic growth was 6 per cent from the 1960s onwards but few Turks were impressed by this. It was not until this level of growth had accumulated for three decades that it became clear that Turkey really was developing a modern economy. In the meantime, an increasingly large urban population began to press for greater rights to receive economic benefits and engage in political participation. The result was a generation of tense social conflicts and confrontations.

October 1973
After two and a half years of military rule, Turkey this month held general elections and they have been won for the first time ever (though not quite with a majority) by the social democrats of Bulent Ecevit's reformed Republican People's Party. Ankara is a city of 1.6 million people. It is now the capital of a country of 38 million people. The Piknik Restaurant, famous for its large glasses of beer and Circassian chicken, is a favourite meeting place.

Just over two decades of competitive party politics have changed the face of Turkey. As a result of policies pursued by the centre-right governments of Süleyman Demirel between 1965 and 1971, the large cities now contain sizeable middle classes and even larger working class districts. The villas with gardens are giving way to streets full of crammed apartment blocks. The days when families walked hand in hand down the boulevard in Ankara on warm evenings are now only a memory. Kızılay is full of jostling crowds these days. In the centre of the square is a large hole, of uncertain purpose, excavated by the mayor, and known to opposition politicians as the 'hole of shame'.

Both the middle classes and the new working class are eager for rapid economic development. In fact since the early 1960s, the Turkish economy has been growing at about 6 per cent a year, one of the highest rates in the OECD area. First generation industrialists in Istanbul are making western consumer goods under licence. This does not please the advocates of economic self-sufficiency on the left who argue that foreign investment will make Turkey weaker not stronger.

In fact, at this time, Turkey's economic links with the outside world are still pretty tenuous. Total foreign trade is only about $2.5 billion or 17 per cent of the national product, below half the OECD average. Traditional farm exports are earning the foreign currency to pay for the new industries. But the foundations of a highly diversified manufacturing sector have been established.

The election victory of the social democrats is the first clear sign that the balance in Turkey is shifting from the countryside to the cities, though it will be another five years before more people live in the towns than on the land. Literacy is not yet universal, though primary education has now been extended throughout the country. Law and order and the fight against terrorism have become major issues. Young people are increasingly polarised between the left and the 'idealist right' and some have even made abortive attempts to start Guevara-style movements in the countryside. They come to nothing.

For most people, consumerism is more important. Black and white television arrived, on a limited basis, about six years earlier. Not everyone has a television yet, even in the metropolis. The 'telesafir', the evening guest who arrives not to enjoy your family's company but hoping to watch your TV, is part of life. Even in the countryside, TV is enthusiastically welcomed. In villages where there is no electricity people learn how to operate a set from tractor batteries. The TV brings vast cultural changes with it as people learn about Caspar the Friendly Ghost or watch Dad's Army and other foreign sitcoms. They also bring advertisements which seem almost tormenting for viewers on low fixed salaries.

There are only four passenger cars per thousand people (compared to 220 in the UK), but the first Turkish passenger cars are now being made. The 1970s will see the horse and cart all but vanish from the streets and roads of Turkey.

By now there is a thriving local music industry in Turkey which has learned how to combine eastern and western themes. Cem Karaca, Zeki Muren, and Ajda Pekkan are among the biggest names.

In October 1973, when the half century of the Republic is celebrated, there are still many people alive who remember its establishment. The high point of the celebrations is the opening of the First Bosphorus Bridge. Soon after the anniversary, the Republic loses one of its main links with the past, when former president İsmet İnönü dies on December 25.

October 1998
There are two Bosphorus Bridges when Turkey celebrates its seventy-fifth anniversary. Ankara has a metro. Istanbul is a megalopolis of nearly 12 million and about the largest city in Europe. Ankara's population is over 3 million.

But Turkey has proved Malthus wrong. Resources have risen faster than the population. The population is now around 63 million, but there are signs that it is slackening fast and that forecasts of the size at which it will eventually stabilise are being downgraded.

Income levels in the cities have risen much faster than anyone would have thought possible in the 1970s. Shortages of water and electricity, a chronic problem in earlier decades, are now much less familiar. It is not so clear that this is happening in the countryside where more than forty percent of the workforce still live. The rise of large urban populations helps accelerate change in the hinterland. In many central Anatolian villages, for example, farmers find that switching to crops such as potatoes brings immediate rewards. As a result of the irrigation projects on the Euphrates, a vast agricultural revolution is underway in southern Turkey.

Infrastructure which hardly existed even in 1973 has been largely completed. Electricity, water, and telephones had arrived in every Turkish village by the end of the 1980s. As a result of road and airport construction, the seaboard of western and southern Turkey has long been opened up to international tourism, bringing for instance around a million Britons to the country each year. The country they visit may look traditional to them but in fact it is now the largest regional economy by far and the eighth largest trading partner of the European Union. It seems poised to remain strong despite crashes in

Russia (since the fall of Communism once more one of Turkey's main trading partners) and South East Asia.

Technology and social change are going hand in hand. Turkey is also the largest regional market for mobile phones. Half a million Turks are on the Internet. There are over twenty national TV channels, most of them belonging to the private sector. In the west of the country, the dream of creating a modern industrial society with a consumer middle class has largely been realised. What is more Turkey is now a trading nation, doing over $40 billion of foreign trade a year. It has a customs union with the European Union, after having successfully dismantled its tariff barriers to competition over 22 years. Turkey is the only country which has been able to do this without financial assistance, something that the Europeans had promised in March 1995, but they do not keep their pledge.

Istanbul, Ankara, and Izmir are now increasingly like big cities anywhere else in Europe, though they have a higher population density per hectare. Consumer tastes have adjusted accordingly with cornflakes and Big Macs in favour among the young. The ice creams you buy for your children are the same brands as you get in England. There are losses as well as gains. Traditional restaurants have been largely wiped out in tourist resorts.

Turkey's middle class has become a business class, travelling abroad in search of opportunities. Not everyone succeeds, but horizons have become global. Turkish television broadcasts to viewers from Central Asia to the Atlantic. Arts and leisure pursuits flourish as never before.

Though the economy still grows by about 6 per cent per year, there is little doubt that it would grow much faster if Turkey could attract more foreign investment. Even so many companies have now spotted the attractions of the Turkish market. Ankara now has two branches of Marks & Spencer, the British department store. Those who wish to do so can buy British Christmas crackers for the New Year festivities.

Like Italy at a comparable level of development, Turkey's economic and social progress has come despite inconclusive general elections, fragile coalitions, and general instability, all of which combine to produce a certain occasional demoralisation. Not everyone appreciates all that has been achieved - which may not be altogether bad, since the appetite for progress and improvement remains strong. But that is no reason to forget basic truths. Advance is possible because the long peace which Atatürk and İnönü began in Turkey in 1923 still continues. When the centenary of the Republic comes round in another quarter of a century, it will be their achievements, then as now, that people will be celebrating.

| 5 |

Development and the Rural Community

Inspired Restraint

Dr David Shankland

To speak before such a distinguished audience is a great privilege. It is doubly so because it provides also an opportunity to celebrate a friend and teacher, Professor Paul Stirling, who, if he had lived, would have addressed us today on this topic. It seems fitting to dedicate this talk to his memory, and to take his long research career as a beginning point for our discussion.

Stirling, one of the most well known of all international commentators on modern Turkey, was particularly noted for the great depth and long time-scale of his ethnographic research. This personal overview made him uniquely qualified to discuss the development of Turkey under the Republic. Indeed, it could be said that Stirling's maturity as a scholar developed hand in hand with Turkey's modernisation, and that he gained a great deal of his insights from observing this rapid social change.

Specifically, Stirling conducted his first research in Turkey in a small village in Kayseri between 1948 and 1950.

He submitted the fruits of this work for his doctorate in 1952, and then returned to Turkey to conduct further research in a slightly larger village, one close by his first. In the following years, he concentrated on university duties in Britain, but was able to return briefly in the 1970s, then for a much longer period in the 1980s, and finally for several summers' research during the 1990s.

This research was written up initially through learned papers, then in his famous monograph *Turkish Village*.[1] As he grew older, he began to piece the rich insights yielded by his long acquaintance with the villagers into a wider synthesis, writing on micro-social change and on issues of development in Turkey. Finally, in a large project brought to fruition just before his death, he placed the accumulated field notes from more than fifty years of research on the world wide web. Annotated carefully, placed within the framework of an advanced data-processing programme and a supplementary photographic record, they enable students from all over the world to gain access to one the most extensive accumulations of ethnographic and social data that has ever been collected.

In his interaction with the scholarly community, Stirling loved above all the small seminar groups, the informal questions that take place after a presentation, and the chance to scythe through vague or imprecise thought that such settings offer. When discussing Turkey, which his long experience enabled him to do with an unparalleled fund of examples, he frequently made one particular point: that the Kemalist reforms, whatever difficulties the Republic may suffer, have been an outstanding success. He did not like bureaucracies. He was certainly alive to the deficiencies and the conflicts that can arise in any society. All this made him acutely wary of becoming an apologist. Nevertheless, he felt that to deny the thorough transformation of the Turkish countryside, the development of the cities into metropolitan communities, the establishment of a transport, communications, educational, health and service infrastructure, the growth in industrial output, the emergence of a modern scholarly community, and the other similar indisputable attributes of a Westernised country was, simply, profoundly mistaken.[2]

In order to appreciate the soundness of such a judgement, it is only necessary to compare the situation at the outset of his research with that today. When Stirling began in his village, named *Sakaltutan*, in 1948, there was no electricity. There was no running water, there was no asphalt road, and there was no access to health facilities. Average life expectancy was about forty. The yield from crops was poor, perhaps no more than twofold, if that, or at best fourfold or fivefold. People were bitterly subject to the vagaries of the weather. If the winter was particularly harsh, they froze. Of course there was a vibrant village community, but the people who inhabited it were continuously reminded of their own mortality. They married young, cultivated children as a support in their old age, expanded their land holdings if they could, expected to work hard, and to die before enjoying greatly the fruits of their labour.

Already, when Stirling had arrived this had begun to change. Some youths were working in the factories in Kayseri in order to supplement their income, and they came to the village at weekends and holidays. The great transformation, though, began after his research had commenced, through the 1950s, 1960s and 1970s. When he returned in 1972, though only briefly, he was astounded at the differences he could see. The village was conspicuously better off, both individually and collectively, via improved health facilities, remittances arriving in the village from migrant labour, vastly improved roads and far greater educational opportunities.[3]

During his later research, he was able to follow the changes in more detail, once more growing close to the community. This time, he was able to trace in detail the fortunes of the migrants who had left the village. He found that they had been absorbed successfully into the large local cities in the south, particularly Adana. There, through their specialisation in the building trade, many had come to own their own homes in the towns. Unemployment among them was low, and some men had done very well indeed.

The overall picture of vastly increased prosperity that Stirling insisted upon is not in any way an isolated phenomenon. One of the closest friends from the area where I researched, a school teacher, was in his youth charged with looking after the family flocks and remembers vividly the excruciating boredom of having to sit looking after them for the whole day before bringing them back at night. He attended the local school, then gained his diploma, attending university throughout the social upheaval of the late seventies. Then, marrying a midwife, he initially lived in a new house provided by the Ministry of Health in his natal village. They saved for a new apartment, built as part of a co-operative in a local town. Moving there, he was able to fill it with books and live in comfort. Then, saving money again, he finally has bought a larger apartment in Ankara, with plenty of room for his family, and is able to play a full part in the intellectual life of the capital.

My friend is not a businessman. He has not made money from writing. Along with his wife, he is simply a hard-working civil servant who has benefited from the far wider changes that have come to Turkish society in the last decades. To understand these changes in detail is exceptionally difficult precisely because of this universality: they affect every aspect of life in Turkey, and cannot be considered only as isolated economic statistics. To take only one very small issue among many that might be chosen, the relationship between rural and urban has profoundly altered. At the commencement of the Republic, Turkey was 86 per cent rural. Industrial production was rudimentary. The cities existed not so much as sources of labour but rather as seats of politics, education and government. Villages existed remote from the cities, and beset with their own specific problems, problems that were inherent within a lifestyle that could organise itself largely without any direct intervention from the administrative centres.

Scepticism and explanation

Stirling was immensely sceptical about the models that are used to explain this transformation. He would point out, for example, that the *gecekondu*, shanty-town, dwellers who form a poor majority in the cities are often held to be a burden on the existing urban environment. He felt that this image of a static pool of impoverished *deracinés* was quite mistaken. Through his detailed statistics in micro-migration, he was able to demonstrate that there very quickly develops a massive economic differentiation among people. Even first-generation migrants were often able not just to better themselves in the towns but also to become extremely successful. By the late eighties, only forty years after his first coming into contact with the village, he found several genuine millionaires had been entered into his database. It is not a complete success story, of course. There are also some people who have not managed to get anywhere, because of some form of illness, difficulty in forming social relationships, or other misfortune. Nevertheless, his extremely detailed study, whilst laborious to conduct, proved that life among even the poorer migrants in Turkey is in fact very mobile: those who have the brains, capability and desire may indeed achieve their aspirations.

Following Stirling's lead in questioning the models that people use to explain social behaviour, I would like to offer a further instance. In explanation of the creation of a new urban heritage, the dominant conception is that of villages emptying rapidly, and the population from them pouring into the cities. Of course this is partly true: Istanbul, Izmir and increasingly Ankara, or even Bursa, appear sometimes that they are bursting at the seams. It is quite understandable that long-established urban dwellers should complain at what they see as the 'villageification' of their environment. However, even a cursory glance at the regional population statistics, or even a short tour around Anatolia shows that this popular conception of the creation of the urban environment through mass migration concentrated on the largest cities is at best only partially true.

In fact, as well as movement into the largest cities, urban life is also very substantially created through the expansion of existing village settlements into towns, and then into cities in their own right. This process is substantially aided by the state, so that a small rural community officially classified '*köy*', may expand to become a municipality, '*belediye*', and then perhaps a district centre, *bucak merkezi*, then a sub-province centre, *ilçe*, and then finally, a provincial centre, *il*, in its own right. In each case, a rise up the official state scale brings with it substantial funds to pay for the establishment of local political institutions (such as a salary for the elected mayor and his or her office staff), and increased infrastructural facilities in the shape of schools, roads, health centres, hospitals, police, energy projects, and universities. Each of these stages has a knock-on effect as the steady influx of wages into the community begins to increase the potential market available to local small retail and construction businesses.

Of course, which of the many villages that are found in any one sub-province that will benefit from this expansion and transformation is not clear at the outset. Most try, but not all may achieve success. However, with luck, political acumen, ambition, drive and business sense many even medium-size villages have moved swiftly to become municipalities. Of these, some will become sub-province centres, even if the ultimate goal of becoming a provincial centre is available only to a few.

Taking into account this possibility of the rural itself becoming urban means that our models of the relationship between rural and city life may become much more dynamic. We should not consider rural life as being isolated but profoundly connected with life in the cities, and in itself changing. Villagers, whilst often trying to move to the city, are at the same time actively trying to emulate city life and to incorporate urban institutions into their rural communities. Contemporary relations between village and city should not be typified as a migratory flow between two fairly static types of society, but rather as an interlocking whole, an intricate pattern in which migration to the large cities is important, but in which the development of rural communities also plays a key role. The Republican state has been, and is, an essential factor in this endeavour: it guides the rural communities, permitting and encouraging them to install infrastructural projects which then become the foundation for the further urbanisation of the rural environment.

The founding of the Republic
Turning now to the founding period of the Republic, is there anything in its initial principles that would enable us to foresee this later pattern of dynamic, widespread expansion of the rural? It is widely held that there is not. The dominant intellectual conception of Turkey's modern history is that during the period prior to 1950, rural life was neglected, and that the increasing frustration of the villagers was one of the reasons for the later sweeping victory of the Democrat Party. As a partial explanation for the electoral victory, this may very well be valid: people in villages clearly felt that the Republican People's Party should be replaced by a different governing group. However, to extrapolate from the desire for change in an electorate to claim that this must mean that the early Kemalists neglected rural life in its entirety is surely too casual and too sweeping. I would argue that, quite the contrary, this early Republican period provided the basis for the subsequent development and expansion of rural life in today's Turkey.

In order to realise this, we need to think of the way that the reforms proceeded in what was then a predominantly rural society. The Republican model was to cajole, to persuade and to illustrate the pattern that modernisation should take. They built factories, dispatched schools teachers, created model farms and, of course, opened the village institutes and hearths designed to pass on their Kemalist message (so well elucidated by Professor Akşin in his paper above). However, they did not adopt the communist model of collectivisation, nor did they seek to destroy the basic cohesion of village life. On the contrary, village law sought to cement the relationship between land and community by insisting that each settlement put aside a substantial parcel of land at its centre that could be used for collective grazing, but could not be ploughed or otherwise taken over. Further land reforms strengthened, rather than threatened, the possibility of poor peasant families acquiring land in their own names by aiming to reduce the size of large land holdings.

That the Kemalists left the villages' social structure intact did not stem from an incapability to disturb their lives (they were undisputed masters of the land and of the armed forces) but was a deliberate, self-conscious action. The more I read and study material from this early period, the more I am convinced that the Republican People's Party and their predecessors had a very clearly worked out rural policy, which was based on development through rural communities' existing social life, and was not intent on destroying it.

That they were able to do this at all depends of course, on the capacity of traditional, subsistence farming communities to absorb modern infrastructure. Very briefly, I would like to outline the way that this appears to be possible. Although village life is not the same all over Turkey, in central and western Anatolia, there is generally a standard type of village organisation, where there is a mosque in the centre of the village and nowadays between 50, 70, or 80 larger households grouped around this mosque in a tight-knit community. Most households own themselves enough land to meet their basic subsistence needs: they expect that they will work on their own land and that they will reap the benefits accordingly. The community also has still a fair amount of pastureland, which is owned collectively. So, village life consists roughly of a number of fairly homogenous, egalitarian economic units which also have a sense of being part of a larger whole, both at the village and national level. There is a very low division of labour, and they work together collectively when needed (even if such labour is largely in exchange for cash rather than the free mutual support that it is said used to be the case).

As the state sought the development of the rural communities, it did so primarily through massive state investment in schools, roads, health, agricultural credits, electricity, water and telecommunications. Throughout this endeavour, as I have stressed, it did not undermine the basic economic freedom of the peasant to survive through their small-holdings but reinforced it, both through the maintenance of agricultural subsidies, and through the successive land law reforms. The infrastructure introduced to the villagers was given to the community as a whole, and often constructed through joint initiatives.[4] This emphasis on the private household alongside the public community is in many ways compatible with traditional village life, whereby the communal centres of mosque, tea-house and market at the centre of the village provide a shared resource for all, and it is not a coincidence that in many villages the state buildings are found in the centre, close to the mosque, mirroring the spatial organisation of the pre-modern period.

I have only indicated in the barest outline why it might be that the agricultural village may integrate with the state, and even flourish as it comes into contact with a monetary economy. To justify this contention in detail would take much more time, though I should stress that other researchers, such as Sirman have made similar findings.[5] Passing on quickly, I would suggest that there is a further benefit of leaving the subsistence household unit and village community intact, even if the system of peasant, extended family farming appears obsolete to the economic advisers employed by the European Union. When people become migrants, being part of an extended household with an economic base means that they remain part of a clear social support network through the relatives that remain in the village. For example, when they are short of money and they cannot afford to maintain their children in the poor accommodation, which is, perhaps, all they can afford in an urban area at that time, they can send their children back to the village to be looked after by their grandparents who still live in the village. They can go back to their villages if they go temporarily bankrupt. In the rural area one does not go bankrupt, one simply 'runs out' of sheep and one borrows a few more from a friend and starts up again. If one is perhaps doing badly in the town having been hit by inflation or exploited by somebody in a poor job, food can be sent from the village to keep one alive until the situation improves. By maintaining what, from an economic point of view, is an outdated mode of production, the Turkish nation has nevertheless gained immensely in flexibility when it is trying to achieve social development as a whole.

To conclude, my idea (stated here only in outline) is this: the accelerating transformation of the rural into urban settlements, and the related social mobility which is now a very important characteristic of Turkish society, derive in great part from the early Republican procedure of allowing the traditional peasant social organisation to flourish within an overall highly developed state-led infrastructural plan. If this model is correct, I submit that it may lead us to rethink the role of the state and the Republican People's Party within the subsequent development of the countryside, and indeed, in the nation as a whole.

Questions from the floor:

Q.   Could you tell us a little about support to the rural community? Could you explain what facilities exist, the extent and significance of the infrastructural services within those communities?

A.   Above all, the state is vital. Nearly all the infrastructural support in villages is provided by the government. This assistance is channelled through different ministries, which are responsible for developing particular aspects. In a village today you can expect to find definitely a primary school, probably a middle school and sometimes even a lycée of some sort. Probably 90 per cent of villages, perhaps more, have electricity. Nearly all have some form of state organised water supply, although that is not always necessary. The state also provides agricultural credits and in almost every village there is a health officer who can help transport villagers to the local hospital if necessary, and that health officer is also usually a midwife. This means that the basics of infrastructural support are present in almost every village in Turkey.

Q.   I would like to ask about the role of the Turkish military in village life. National service affects just about everybody. Young men are taken from remote parts of the country and moved perhaps even abroad. This must have an influence on social progress.

A.   The idea of studying the effect of long periods of conscription on young people is an important one. I wonder sometimes whether some of the bitter social discontinuities of the 1970s were not partly caused by the fact that if everybody in the country is trained how to shoot, they may actually carry on doing so after they come back from their military service. Leaving this thought to one side, I accept of course that the theme of the Turkish army being a modernising influence must also be valid because people conscripted, if they do not know already, learn how to read and to write, and they also have basic history lessons about the background to the Turkish Republic.

One further impression: in my experience it seems that when youths come back from military service they reintegrate quickly into the previous family units and social networks. So while they may have gained personally by the experience they have had in the army, conscription itself does not impact largely on the wider fabric of Turkish society. This is only a passing idea: it would be good to see a research project on this topic.

Q.   As to one of the social consequences of this mobility, and with reference to the phrase Andrew Mango used about 'vibrant dynamism', 'people moving to the cities in large numbers', 'going where the bright lights are, where the work is', in a city like Istanbul, or the greater Istanbul area (which has the same population as the whole of Greece) is there any evidence that two kinds of religion have emerged from this mobility? Is there such a thing now in Turkey as a rural Islam and an urban politicised Islam? And, are you concerned about that?

A.   To answer the last part of your question first: I am concerned. However, I do not think that there is a separate urban and rural Islam because one of the consequences of the migration and the rapid expansion of the cities and villages is that there is no clear boundary between urban and rural life in modern Turkey. Consequently, the politicisation of Islam is not solely an urban phenomenon. The Welfare Party had a superb organisation, an organisation that extended deep into rural as well as urban life. It meant that it was able to recruit individual agents in almost every village. It possessed a direct hierarchical infrastructure. This meant that a manager in this particularly religious party could be sitting in Ankara yet could pass a particular piece of information on, or learn something about, any village in Turkey by simply asking that particular man, one's agent, in that particular village, whose responsibilities included recruiting more sympathisers. And so there is a type of continuity of political Islam, which is not dependent on a rural or urban boundary.

Q.   As far as mobility is concerned, one of the main impacts on Sakaltutan, Stirling's village, was the mobility between Germany and Sakaltutan. This has had an enormous impact on social change and social life in the village. In Germany today, there are about half a million Turkish school children going to schools in Germany. But the statistics are shocking. Out of half a million, only 800 Turkish students are allowed to go to *Gymnasium*, which is the way though to university. But the remaining, a large population, have to go to *Real Schule* or to others. I wonder if you have any point to raise about this.

A.   Unfortunately, I cannot comment on that, although it sounds very unfortunate, because I am not a specialist in the Turkish diaspora in Germany.

Q.   You have just said that you do not think that there was a difference between rural and urban Islamism. As someone, who has studied the Welfare Party itself, I can guarantee that they have two separate organisations. These are separate in how they move in rural and urban areas.
       About the Republican Party and 1948, one of the reasons why, in 1948, 1949 and 1950 the Democrat Party finally came to power, was because of the great dislike felt for the Republican Party by the villagers. In all the documents available on this subject, none contain evidence of a coherent policy towards the Turkish villagers. There was one very good and very coherent thing that the government did at the time, and that was to establish the People's Houses, which actually played a part, later, in the emergence of great authors like Yaşar Kemal, and Kemal Tahir.

A.   Of course the Welfare Party must have organisations in the urban and rural spheres and, by definition, they must work differently in these different areas, but there does not seem to be a boundary. In other words one can find people in the most remote village with the most sophisticated political Islamic ideology. Likewise, in the heart of the town one can find someone wearing rural gear still, bearing the most rustic interpretations of Islam.

You are right of course that at the moment academia says that the Republican government had no coherent policy towards rural life. However, the point of my paper is that I think that this is one area that we should look at again. It is quite clear that the Republic possessed some sort of policy. They did not, for example, take the collectivisation model, as they did in the Soviet Union which killed millions of people. In addition, there is no doubt that the early Republicans developed a self-conscious, deliberate policy that was aimed at reforming rural life. They did so within certain well-set parameters that avoided disrupting the basic unit of Sunni village life. Simply put, this inspired restraint is, in my opinion, one of the keys to the later success that the Republic now enjoys.

Q.   Although it is dangerous to compare, if one looks at other societies, particularly in the Balkans, large numbers of people moved to the cities. They supported their fellow villagers, but this long-term social linking has tended to decay over one or two generations. How vibrant are the village communities in Turkey? Is that a potential problem? Will they remain?

A.   One of the fascinating things about modern Turkey is the simple little statistic: 1923, 86 per cent rural, 1993, 60 per cent urban - a massive transformation! How did it come about? It partly came through migration but only very partly. It came most of all through villages changing themselves into cities so they created the urban on a rural panorama. How is that accomplished? By leaving the basic community intact. A small village has perhaps a hundred households. It wants to get richer. It attracts state infrastructure through persuasion, through political means, through simple luck because of a new state policy. As the state infrastructure increases and health gets better, the population grows. If they are fortunate they can become then a municipality. Some of the municipalities get changed into sub-province centres. The sub-province centres ultimately get changed into provincial centres. They may need all sorts of political machinations to get on that road but nevertheless it means that 20 or 30 years down the line any small basic little community can, depending on a combination of fortuitous circumstances, become a large flourishing town and perhaps even a city. So, the potential for change is always there. It is not a question simply of rural areas emptying to existing urban sites.

This means that some villages will do more than survive, they will grow in their own right. A few will wither and become dormitories for older villagers who have come back to retire. Others will fall below the minimum needed to maintain a community and will become deserted. It should not be seen as a uniform, or simple process, but one that can only be evaluated by looking at each region, and each settlement on a case by case basis.

Q.   The status of a women in Istanbul and in other big cities has clearly changed. I wonder what the situation is in village life?

Q.   My question is similar, you have painted a very seductive picture of all these movers and shakers, moving into Turkish cities and doing their thing and being very successful, but I wish to ask also what of the silent majority - the women?

A.   Professor Stirling used to say that there was a slow steady discernible improvement in the lot of women. In other words, that women in 1948 were treated very, very poorly. Even though some Turkish men today might maintain that they are good old-fashioned Turkish men and do not believe in feminism, *ipso facto*, there has been an enormous improvement in the position of women, both politically and economically. One final point is that in Britain we are finding that girls, are now doing far better in school examinations than boys. Curiously enough, they found the same phenomenon in Turkey some years ago. Even in rural Turkey some girls are going to school. The moment you get to a small town setting, girls shoot ahead of boys in the school tests, and again in the university entrance exams. So, it is possible that the future of Turkey lies with the women.

| 6 |

Turkey and Cyprus

Professor Clement Dodd

In the House of Commons a short while ago there was a debate on Cyprus in which the preponderance of opinion was pro-Greek Cypriot.[1] It was hardly a distinguished debate. Almost every speaker showed only a partial understanding of the Cyprus issue and a great deal of bias. It was interesting that support for the Greek Cypriot position came from both sides of the House, whilst only Conservative Party members spoke up for the Turkish Cypriots. Like all House of Commons debates it was confrontational, a tradition that itself inhibits understanding. Labour Party support for the Greek Cypriot cause is not unusual; it reflects in part the Labour Party's traditional support for colonial subjects struggling to be free. Moreover the Cypriot left were prominent in that struggle.

Conservative support is more difficult to understand. Like some Labour Party members they are, of course, under pressure from Greek Cypriot constituents, who are well organised. Also they too have been subject to carefully orchestrated Greek Cypriot publicity for their cause. Conservative members may also perhaps be more sympathetic to the Greek Cypriot side by virtue, in some cases, of an education that has always accorded a special place to classical Greece as the inspiration for modern civilisation. Among many liberals, and indeed among conservatives, there is also sympathy for the liberal tradition that regards the Ottoman Empire, and by extension modern Turkey, as heavy handed, if not oppressive. But most important of all is undoubtedly the fact that Britain has two important sovereign bases in Cyprus that rely to a good degree for their smooth operation on the goodwill of the Greek Cypriots. Yet among some conservatives must also be some unease that since 1960 conservative governments have seen fit to support the Greek Cypriot rather than the Turkish Cypriot side in the Cyprus issue, despite the fact that Britain was one of the Guarantors of the 1960 settlement, which the Greek Cypriots overthrew between 1963 and 1965. This is loyalty to government policy that has consistently denied, in effect, that the Turkish Cypriots have right on their side. All British governments have supported the Greek Cypriots in their claim to be the legitimate government of the Republic of Cyprus with sovereignty over the North.

One of the facets of Greek publicity for their case is that between 1400 and 1200 BC Cyprus was almost predominantly Greek in culture, despite rule by many foreign invaders over the centuries, Persian, Roman, Latin, Venetian, Ottoman, or British. In this scenario Turkey has no more claim to interest in the island than any of the other sometime rulers. Coupled with this is the Greek Cypriot view that Turkey is no more than an aggressor which intervened for her own interests in 1974 under pretence of coming to the aid of the Turkish Cypriots, who merit nothing more than minority status under Greek Cypriot rule.

On the outbreak of the First World War Britain annexed Cyprus, having leased it from the Ottomans since 1878. With the outbreak of the war the position of the Turkish Cypriots became difficult. They were obliged to become British subjects unless they chose to leave the island.

It is true that there has been a long history of Greek culture and Greek Orthodox Christianity in the island which survives to this day. It is not always appreciated, however, that the Ottomans did not just come in 1571 to conquer and rule the island; they also colonised it with Turks from Anatolia. Nor is it always appreciated that Cyprus is only forty miles away from Turkey and could dominate the important ports in southern Turkey. These two factors in themselves explain Turkey's continuing interest in the affairs of the island.

To expand a little on history, it has to be noted, first, that the Ottomans captured the island not from the Greek Cypriots but from the Venetians. The first impact of this conquest was to liberate the Greek Cypriots. Under Latin and Venetian rule they had for centuries been much oppressed. Under Ottoman rule they became relatively free. They were freed from serfdom when the feudal system was abolished. They also became almost autonomous in managing the affairs of their own church and community in accordance with the Ottoman Way of treating non-Muslim subject communities (*millets*) as largely self governing under their religious leaders.

Secondly, some thirty thousand Turks were settled in the island, mostly by the enforced transfer of peasant farmers, artisans and nomads from Turkey. Farmers were allocated lands left vacant by the effects of war and deprivation and previous maladministration. In addition Ottoman officials were brought in to govern the new acquisition of empire. Significantly, the Ottomans were always more involved in government than in commerce or industry and did not try to establish an economic elite. Commerce was left to Greek and other Cypriots. It would appear from various reports that the population of the island was more or less evenly divided between Greek and Turkish Cypriots, with the Turks probably in the majority in the early years of the Ottoman conquest. By the end of the nineteenth century, however, the first (British) census showed the Greek Cypriots to outnumber the Turkish Cypriots by three to one.[2]

Nevertheless it is clear that the Turkish Cypriots have grounds for considering themselves an integral part of the population and an equal partner in an island they both ruled and colonised. It has been noted that while this tradition of Ottoman rule left non-Muslim communities free to acquire wealth and social prominence, the Turkish Cypriots, as former rulers, have always 'evinced an instinctive hostility to anything which smacked of Greek political supremacy'.[3]

With the outbreak of the war the position of the Turkish Cypriots became difficult. They were obliged to become British subjects unless they chose to leave the island. In 1925 the island was declared a British colony, when there was much discussion between Britain and Turkey on the legal status of those Turkish Cypriots who wished to leave.[4]

The inter-war period is particularly apposite to the theme of this book. It is moreover a period when it is often believed that Turkey had little or no interest in Cyprus, and when there was allegedly little or no stirring of Turkish national feeling on the island.[5] What does clearly emerge, on the contrary, is that Ankara watched Cypriot affairs very closely indeed. Apart from making forcible representations on the subject of the nationality of emigrants to Turkey, a very complex legal issue in which Ankara appeared to have the better case, a close watch was kept on Greek Cypriot demands for *enosis*. A special study was made in Ankara of the 1931 uprising against the British. Also the Turkish Cypriots complained to Ankara about the severity of British rule, and in particular of the development of British administrative and financial control of the religious foundations (*evkaf*).

Also they complained that the British authorities relied upon, and consulted as leaders of the Turkish Cypriot community, the traditional Muslim elite, neglecting the young Turkish Cypriots who were becoming more and more influenced by Kemalism. By ignoring, and to a degree proscribing, Kemalism, the British authorities helped greatly to develop it in its modernist and nationalist aspects. This was plain to see when a visit by a Turkish warship to Famagusta in 1938 attracted thousands of enthusiastic Turkish Cypriots from all over the island. The British had put the blame for the manifestations of Turkish nationalism on to a small number of activists, but demonstrations of this sort showed how wrong they were. The British did not want to encourage Turkish nationalism lest it presented them with another nationalist movement that the Governor, oddly, believed would coalesce with the Greek Cypriot nationalist movement against the British.

Despite the active discouragement of the spread of Kemalism among the Turkish Cypriots by the British authorities, the Turkish Government was very circumspect in seeking not to upset the British, whose support Kemal Atatürk was anxious to obtain. The Turkish Government was intent on not being seen to challenge British rule in Cyprus, with which they were well content. When Britain asked in Ankara that the current Turkish Consul in Cyprus be requested to be a little less actively Kemalist he was promptly removed from office by Ankara!

In the 1950s the intensification of the *enosis* campaign (especially after the beginning of the EOKA terrorism in 1955) was one of the factors that brought Turkey out more fully in support of the Turkish Cypriots. It was also a time when Greece sought to internationalise the dispute and came out strongly for self-determination for the island, a process that would have left the Turkish Cypriots in a permanent minority. In addition, Turkey now began to doubt Britain's determination to hold on to Cyprus, especially after the weakness of Britain was revealed by the Suez crisis.

Ankara held its hand until the mid-1950s, though as early as 1949 the Turkish Government informed the British Foreign office that Turkey would be fundamentally concerned if a change of sovereignty were envisaged in Cyprus.[6] This no doubt reflected increased Turkish Cypriots' anxieties evident in the 1940s and which found expression in the Turkish press and in pro-Turkish Cypriot demonstrations in Ankara. As the situation worsened in the mid-1950s, and some EOKA attacks on Turkish Cypriots occurred, the Turkish Foreign Minister stressed Turkey's strategic interests in the island and supported not self-determination, but *taksim*, a division of the island, the word on everybody's lips in Ankara. It was well nigh impossible given the geographical intermixture of Greek and Turkish Cypriots. When Britain seemed, with the Radcliffe proposals (1956), to be veering in the direction of self-determination, Turkey was distinctly uneasy, but was reassured by the statement by Alan Lennox Boyd, the British Colonial Secretary (19 December 1956) that 'any exercise of self-determination should be effected in such a manner that the Turkish Cypriot community shall be given freedom to decide for themselves their future. In other words Her Majesty's Government recognise that the exercise of self-determination in such a mixed population must include partition'.

In 1958 the British Government presented the MacMillan plan, which provided for a degree of self-government, but not self-determination, with the participation of Greek and Turkish Representatives in the council which had authority for major matters of government and which was chaired by the Governor. It was turned down by the Greek Cypriots and by the Greek Government, though accepted, if not with enthusiasm, by the Turkish side, since it did not provide for partition. In the House of Commons' debate on the Macmillan Plan, which was favourably received there (26 June 1958), MacMillan stated that if the British Government was 'thrown back on other solutions the Government would stand by its pledges, including that contained in the statement which the Colonial Secretary made on 19 December 1956'.

These two statements are dear to the hearts of the Turkish Cypriots and clearly owe much to the vigorous Cyprus policy adopted by the Turkish Foreign Minister, Fatin Rüstü Zorlu and the Prime Minister, Adnan Menderes In the upshot it was not the MacMillan Plan, but an 'independence' solution that was adopted. It was worked out by Greece and Turkey in a series of meetings in 1959. This was a solution that Greece and the Greek Cypriots regarded as second best to self-determination, but infinitely better than the Macmillan Plan, with its formal enlistment of Turkish participation in the administration of the island. The agreements made established the principles of a Constitution for an independent state. The Greek and Turkish Cypriots agreed to this solution, the Greek Cypriots reluctantly. Britain satisfied her security needs under the new agreements by the acquisition of two bases under British sovereignty. The new Republic of Cyprus was guaranteed by Britain, Greece and Turkey under a Treaty of Guarantee (1960) which allowed for the right of intervention by the Guarantor Powers, separately or jointly, if it was needed to restore the state of affairs established by the Basic (unalterable) Articles of the Constitution.

Turkish policy after 1960 was less forthright and self-assured than under Menderes and Zorlu. After the 1960 military coup in Turkey the government set up under the veteran İsmet İnönü did not cope satisfactorily with the threat to the 1960 Cyprus Constitution. This occurred when the Greek Cypriots resorted to violence to force the Turkish Cypriots to acquiesce in Greek Cypriot predominance in government after the latter had intimated, and Ankara had declared, that they rejected constitutional changes that would have effectively reduced the Turkish Cypriots to minority status. Concerned to stop the violence against the Turkish Cypriots, Ankara did not pay sufficient heed to the dangers inherent in UN Security Council Resolution No. 186 of 4 March 1964. This Resolution provided for a UN Force to keep the peace, but by its recognition of the purely Greek Cypriot government then in office (after all Turkish Cypriots had been forced out by the violence) in effect recognised that rump government as the legitimate government of the Republic of Cyprus.[7]

It is clear that the Turkish Government did not sufficiently appreciate the importance of the wording of the Resolution; it has resulted in recognition by all states, save Turkey, of the Greek Cypriot administration as the legitimate government of the Republic of Cyprus. As violence continued against the Turkish Cypriots, despite the presence of the UN Force, in 1964 Turkey threatened military intervention (which it would have found difficult to mount for shortage of landing craft) but was bluntly warned against the venture by President Lyndon Johnson in what was a major and deeply resented international rebuff for Turkey.

In 1967 Turkey threatened action again when attacks on the Turkish Cypriots continued, with the result that some 12000 Greek troops left the island, as did Grivas, the guerrilla leader who had returned from Greece to establish EOKA-B to attack the Turkish Cypriots. As a result, the economic blockades of Turkish Cypriot enclaves (to which they had mostly withdrawn for self-defence) were lifted. This was a victory for Turkey, but did not bring about the return of the Turkish Cypriots to their proper place in government.[8]

From 1967 to 1974, in liaison with Greece, Turkey sought to bring about a revised constitutional settlement between the Greek and Turkish Cypriots. Under severe pressure as a result of their distressing economic and social conditions, and without outright support for their cause by Ankara, the Turkish Cypriots were obliged to consider concessions that would have greatly worsened their situation by comparison with that obtaining under the 1960 Constitution.[9] However, the Greek junta's influence in Greek Cypriot politics resulted in the Nicos Sampson coup that ousted Makarios also brought about Turkish military intervention in 1974 designed to prevent *enosis* and to protect the Turkish Cypriots. A year earlier, the accession to power of Bülent Ecevit in coalition with Necmettin Erbakan's religious National Salvation Party had marked a new determination by the Turkish Government to protect the Turkish Cypriots and advance their cause.

Since 1974 Northern Cyprus has been firmly supported by Turkey, though with less enthusiasm at some times than at others. In 1983, just before the newly elected government under Turgut Özal took over power from the military, the Turkish Federated State in Cyprus, as the new Turkish Cypriot state was called, declared itself to be the Turkish Republic of Northern Cyprus. This move was not much welcomed by the new government, anxious to see the Cyprus problem removed from the international agenda. Özal subsequently strove hard for agreement with Greece and attempted in 1991 to arrange a quadripartite conference to be attended by Turkey, Greece, the Greek Cypriot state and the Turkish Republic of Northern Cyprus though without success. He became irritated with Denktaş from time to time, blaming him for the failure of the quadripartite talks initiative, saying: 'The Turkish Cypriots can prefer what they like, but we have made great sacrifices and are continuing to do so. They should appreciate the value of this. We spend more than $200 million a year on Cyprus. This will go on, but a solution has to be found. Cyprus is getting in the way of Turkey's ambitions'.[10] Nevertheless Özal had supported Denktaş at crucial times, as, for instance, in 1988 when he told George Vassiliou, who, as Greek Cypriot President, wanted to discuss Cyprus with him that the person appropriate for him to address was Denktaş. Yet for Özal's international ambitions Cyprus was an obstacle, particularly for his desire to see Turkey as a member of the European Economic Communities, as the European Union then was.

Much the same may be said of Mrs Tansu Çiller. She, too, reflecting the ambitions of certain important sections of the business community, and the western orientated elite, wanted to move closer to Europe. In her case the objective, in 1995, was to conclude a Customs Agreement with the European Union. Her government was much criticised in Turkey because it concluded the Customs Agreement knowing that the EU could only do so by accepting EU accession negotiations for Cyprus. Without this acceptance Greece would have vetoed the Customs Union. The opposition parties in Turkey, led by Mesut Yılmaz and Bülent Ecevit, and many others, severely censured Çiller for providing an opportunity for the EU to accept negotiations with the 'Republic of Cyprus' which illegally claimed authority over the whole island, and despite the undertaking by the Republic of Cyprus in the Treaty of Guarantee (1960), 'not to participate, in whole, or in part, in any political or economic union with any State whatsoever'. Turkey's passive role was deplored. The Çiller government laid itself open to further criticism when, also in 1995, the National Handball Team was allowed by the Sports Minister to play in South Cyprus and, worse perhaps, was allowed to travel via Israel instead of crossing over from the North to the South, which the Greek Cypriot Government would not have allowed.

This ambivalence in Turkish attitudes reflects a certain indifference discernible in some Turkish circles to the Cyprus issue and a desire to be free of it, though mostly support for Turkey's 'baby state' is pronounced, especially at times of seeming crisis in the fortunes of the Turkish Cypriots. For instance, in 1993, Denktaş was disinclined to accept without qualification the Confidence-building measures urged upon him by the UN. In Ankara he received a tumultuous welcome from the Turkish Grand National Assembly when he explained the position and the pressures he had been subjected to by the United Nations. It was a reception only marred by articles in the largest circulation newspaper, *Sabah*, accusing Denktaş of opportunism and of attempting to influence Turkish public opinion over the heads of the Turkish Government.

Recent Turkish support
Since 1995, with the demise of the Çiller government, official Turkish support, and Turkish public opinion, have rallied massively to the Turkish Cypriot cause. This has been due to a number of factors. In the first place, there has been renewed Greek Cypriot aggressiveness, as evidenced by the 1996 demonstrations on the border in Cyprus, which had tragic results. The attempt to pull down a Turkish flag inflamed nationalist sentiment in Turkey. Secondly, and more important,

the intention of the Greek Cypriots to import Russian made S-300 surface to air missiles alarmed the Turkish Government as well as the public. Thirdly the development of a Defence Doctrine between Greece and Greek Cyprus, together with the building of an air base in Paphos to be used by Greek planes increased military tensions. Also in January 1996 Turkey and Greece seemed about to come to blows over who owned the tiny islet of Imia/Kardak just off Turkey's Aegean coast.

In addition to actions of this sort that seemed to challenge Turkish pride and military power, there were other reasons for Turkey's firm support for Northern Cyprus. The application by the Greek Cypriots to join the EU on behalf of the whole island was an affront to the Turkish Cypriots. Secondly, Turkey was in effect told in December 1997 that its chances of entering the EU were very slim; consequently there was little or nothing to gain from Ankara's seeking to persuade Northern Cyprus to make concessions to the Greek Cypriots for the sake of some agreement. This rebuff by the EU coincided with the rise to power of the religious party under Erbakan, and later of Mesut Yılmaz and Bülent Ecevit.

Turkish support for the TRNC has been underlined recently in three joint declarations covering co-operation in a number of areas. The important Turkey-TRNC Declaration of Solidarity (20 January 1997), which was directed mainly to matters of defence, was immediately endorsed by the Turkish Grand National Assembly (21 January). In its Resolution the Assembly extended its support to the principle of the sovereign equality of the two sides in the dispute, and stressed the illegality of the Greek Cypriots' application to the European Union. The Assembly also declared Turkey's intention to develop closer economic links, (notwithstanding Turkey's Customs Union with the EU) and to provide full representation of Turkish Cypriot interests in the international diplomatic arena.[11]

This recent unwavering support by Turkey has encouraged the TRNC to insist that any future UN sponsored negotiations must be on a state-to-state basis. The TRNC will no longer be prepared to be regarded as a 'community' whilst the Greek Cypriot 'community' is regarded outside the negotiations as a state and, worse, as a state whose claims to sovereignty over the TRNC are accepted by all states save Turkey.

In the resulting impasse the Turkish government has worked, and is working, closely and in full accord with that of the TRNC. In August 1998 Turkey endorsed the TRNC's call for a confederation, not for the federation that is called for by the UN and demanded by the Greek Cypriot side.[12] The recent, April 1999, general elections in Turkey have, if anything, increased the level of Turkish political support for Northern Cyprus. The new government is headed by Ecevit and is a coalition of his Democratic Left Party, the Nationalist Action Party, whose nationalism is pronounced, and the Motherland Party, which, under Yılmaz, has always supported the Turkish Cypriots. The Turkish Government recently condemned the UN Security Council's request that the Secretary-General should call together the two leaders for negotiations, a request made earlier by the G-8 meeting, on the grounds that the Security Council still referred to the Greek Cypriot Government as the 'Government of Cyprus'.[13]

In Resolution 1250 the Security Council (29 June 1999) envisaged meetings of the two leaders on any subject (a flexible approach that admitted, it would seem, of confederation as a discussible subject) but in a second Resolution the Council reaffirmed its position that 'a Cyprus settlement must be based on a State of Cyprus with a single sovereignty and international personality and a single citizenship containing two equal communities in a bi-communal and bi-zonal federation'. This suggests renewed forays into the minefield of constitution making for a federation despite lack of success in the past. One difficulty is that the most that can be said of sovereignty in federations is that it is shared among a number of interacting institutions that make up a federal state and is, at best, a composite sovereignty. A more legalistic analysis claims that sovereignty is not *shared* but *divided* among the states composing the federation and the federal authorities, with functions like those of foreign affairs, defence and, say, health, being considered federal. This is a view that has found some favour with the Turkish Cypriots, but their main approach seems to be that in a federation each constituent state should retain its sovereignty, transferring only *functions or powers*, not any part of its sovereignty, to central federal institutions – an approach developed by John Calhoun in the nineteenth century.[14] Interestingly the recent Turkish Cypriot proposal for a confederation (in which equal partnership and unanimity in decision making are notable features) makes reference to powers and functions and not to sovereignty. The preference for a confederation harks back to the most important features of the 1960 Constitution, namely the virtual requirement of unanimity in voting for legislation on major matters in the House of Representatives and in major decisions in the Council of Ministers.

Since constitution making is fraught with difficulties it would seem more profitable to encourage the two sides to come together to solve the major concrete problems with which they are each faced. The TRNC badly needs to be recognised internationally: the international embargo is seriously holding back what could be a prosperous economy, particularly with regard to the development of international tourism. The Greek Cypriots need to have some territory returned, including Varosha, and need a satisfactory settlement of property claims. This could be a win-win negotiation, but it would need great political strength for a Greek Cypriot government to withdraw its claims to sovereignty over Northern Cyprus, as the Irish Government did over Northern Ireland. It is also difficult to imagine that the Greek Cypriots would accept any arrangements that did not include a constitutional settlement along federal lines, though such a federal solution would clearly have to have a large confederal element.

Turkey is firmly behind the TRNC and is now too strong and important to be used with much hope of success as a lever to induce the Turkish Cypriots to make concessions to Greek Cypriot views. In earlier days, when Turkish support was less wholehearted, and the international situation more favourable, the Greek Cypriots did not seem to pay sufficient regard to those elements in Turkish society anxious for a compromise on Cyprus. A hostile and aggressive approach has not produced dividends, but instead has helped solidify Turkish support for the Turkish Republic of Northern Cyprus.

Questions from the floor:

Q.   The professor did not mention offshore banking as one reason why South Cyprus is so prosperous. Incidentally, may I urge members here, who want an enjoyable holiday, to go to North Cyprus while they can?

A.   I am glad you mentioned the question of offshore companies which, as I understand, will be seriously affected if South Cyprus becomes a member of the European Union. An acquaintance of mine has been urging the North to make efforts to attract off-shore companies, some of whom, as I understand, are considering making plans to move to Northern Cyprus.

Q.   I agree with you about the need for recognition of the TRNC. On another point, perhaps you could explain why it is so important for Britain to continue to have bases on Cyprus.

A.   At a recent conference a military expert explained that the British bases in Cyprus are important both for Britain and for NATO. This is, because (1) they have important repair workshops for military equipment, (2) they are staging posts for personnel and material *en route* to trouble spots in, say, the Middle East, (3) they have extensive electronic surveillance facilities, which, it is said, have recently been expanded.

The presence of these bases probably makes it difficult for the major Western powers, and particularly for Britain, to withdraw recognition of the Greek Cypriot Government as sovereign over the whole island. Such an action would no doubt result in serious demonstrations in the South against the bases and against British and other residents in the South. The operation of the bases could become very difficult, I am told, if they were surrounded by a hostile population, whose passions would have been aroused. It will be remembered that in 1974 the American Ambassador to Cyprus was assassinated. The nationalist element in the South should not be underrated and Clerides relies on nationalist support. It would therefore seem to be hazardous for, say, Britain or the United States to declare that they do not recognise the government of the South as the government of the whole island. The way forward would appear to be for the international community to persuade the Greek Cypriots that it would be greatly to their advantage to withdraw their claim to sovereignty over the North (which they will never exercise) in return for territory, a settlement of the property issue and agreement on levels of security. The way would then be open to further co-operation.

Q.   That is one of the most optimistic things we have heard on Cyprus for a long time. You talked of the Cyprus issue being locked up really by the historic mistake of Europe's attitude at the Luxembourg Conference. Ever since then every politician, except Mrs Çiller, has been visiting Northern Cyprus and Turkish military and public opinion have been very supportive of the integration of Northern Cyprus with Turkey. One of the remarkable developments this month was that the European Union's report on Turkey was actually an intelligent, well-written and mature document, unlike the report on Cyprus, which defined the Cyprus problem in ways that one would not allow a student to do. If this means that there is a perspective on membership for Turkey, then is there anything that Turkey will be able to do in meeting Greek Cypriot fears about its army? This is, after all, the main problem from the Greek Cypriot point of view, just as recognition is the main problem from the Turkish Cypriot point of view.

Leading on from the European Union's new attitude to Turkey, if one actually confronts this consensus in Greece and in Cyprus of not wanting to talk about what they would like to do to get peace (because that would destroy their political harmony at home), one has the beginnings of movement and real talk instead of this wretched repetition of formulae, like 'just and lasting peace', which means that nobody has to think about anything.

A.   The softening in the attitude of the EU to Turkey may well be important, but in the report to which you referred the small section on Cyprus still states that Turkey is responsible for the Cyprus situation and should do something about it. In that respect the report did not favour Turkey. The report generally did not provide any incentive to induce Turkey to exert pressure on the Turkish Cypriot Government. As it emerges from the report that EU membership for Turkey is a long way off, there seems little reason for Turkey to seek to influence Northern Cyprus in ways that would meet with the approval of the European Union.

It is difficult to see that the EU's report in any way encourages Turkey to reduce troop levels in Northern Cyprus. Incidentally, there are many guesses about the numbers of Turkish troops in Northern Cyprus, but as Mümtaz Soysal explained at a recent conference, no official figures are ever given. In deciding force levels in northern Cyprus Turkey has to bear in mind the large number of reserve troops in the South of the island. In principle there would seem to be no difficulties on the Turkish side to agreed reductions in personnel and armaments, but it would seem unrealistic to expect any such agreement when the Greek Cypriots continue to import heavy Russian tanks and are planning to import SAM 300 missiles from Russia. Each side fears aggression by the other.

Q.   The talk was a wise and very practical analysis of the situation. It is only to be hoped that the governments involved take notice of it. I have no confidence that they will. One factor not mentioned was the Greek Orthodox Church. I happen to think that when nobody goes to church in Southern Cyprus, then there will be a chance of settling the Cyprus problem, but not until then. The international community is trying to bring the two peoples of Cyprus together, but some confidence-building measures are necessary first. These are not confidence-building measures between Turkish Cypriots and Greek Cypriots, but between Turkish Cypriots and the international community. This is necessary because the Turkish Cypriots have no confidence in the international community, as is the case between themselves and the Greek Cypriots. They have no confidence that the international community is either able or willing to deliver on its promises. As to impartiality, it is common knowledge that since UN Security Council Resolution 186 (4 March 1964) the international community has accepted the Greek Cypriots as the government of the whole island, to which, of course, they have no right. This gives them enormous political and economic advantages, including, for example, the embargo.

As far as treaties are concerned, can one really expect the Turkish Cypriots to place the lives of their families in international assurances, international guarantees, and even international military forces, when the international community failed to protect their constitutional right to life in 1963, 1967 and 1974? And when, even today, the European Union, including Britain, simply brushes aside the 1960 Treaty which prohibits the accession of Cyprus to the European Union? Finally, the Turkish Cypriots are accused of putting forward the precondition that they want recognition. It seems that the only precondition, however, is the insistence of the international community that the Turkish Cypriots should continue negotiating on the basis of the old UN formula (which they have been trying for twenty-five years) and which is going absolutely nowhere. That precondition needs to be removed before any progress can be made.

Q.   I would like to stick to the discipline of asking a question because I think that it is more useful for this discussion. I should like to ask Professor Dodd, if he would cast his mind forward in some way, and fit what he has told us into a framework of a European Union, which has already been enlarged to cover the fast track applicants (including Cyprus - a distinct possibility) not even in ten years' time but beyond that. Could he say what status the north of Cyprus would then have in the European Union? Is he suggesting that in those circumstances, that entity would be accepted as a member of the European Union, a separate member of the European Union? Does he think that is practical politics?

And also what does he think are the implications of the fact that Turkey and that entity would then be in the European Union with Greece and the other part of the island and the whole of the *acquis communitaire* would then apply to it? Does not that make a lot of what is being talked about here sound a little bit *vieux jeux*? It is all going to be a little out of date in the long run. But it is going to be very difficult to resolve if it is approached in this piecemeal way. So I would like to hear his views on that.

Q.   My question is: are human rights the priority for nations, or are the political interests of nations the first priority? And if human rights are the first priority, is it the case that human rights are being given priority when Turkish

Cypriots' rights are disregarded by the imposition of an embargo on them? What does the European Community gain by this embargo?

Q.   It is not correct to say, as one questioner has done, that Professor Dodd was optimistic. Professor Dodd simply set out a possibility, and I would like to know whether he is indeed optimistic. In a sense, the solution of the situation in the Eastern Mediterranean is dependent on the initiative, or at least, the assent of Greek Cyprus, and Greek Cyprus is a prisoner of the past. Recent miscalculations are not the only miscalculations that have occurred in this matter. The miscalculations start in the mid-1950s with the recourse to violence. Violence did not produce *enosis*. Then there was the rejection of the sensible Radcliffe proposals in 1967-57. That did not produce *enosis*. Then there was the abuse of the Constitution of 1960. That did not produce the expected result. We shall leave 1974 on one side. Then there was, in 1974 (the Geneva talks) the rejection of the Turkish proposal for six Turkish Cypriot cantons. That was rejected and produced the division of the island. More recently, we have had the threat of the missiles. Prisoners of all these previous miscalculations are not likely to avoid a further miscalculation, but this is the question I would like Professor Dodd to answer. Is he optimistic?

Q.   My question is almost exactly the same as an earlier one. If the Republic of Cyprus (i.e. the southern part of the island, or two thirds of the island) is admitted as a full member of the European Union, what do you think is going to happen to the north?

Q.   I believe that the Greeks do not want any solution of the Cyprus issue, because they believe they have nothing to gain. They have a lot to gain, however, by maintaining the present tension because they thus appear as victims of Turkish aggression, and they have a lot to play for in the international community, including the EU, which is a very good forum for them.

Q.   Professor Dodd seems to suggest that Britain, and indeed other guarantor powers, should now sit back and say, 'Look, we have done what we can – it is up to you now' and put the ball into the Republic or Greek Cypriot court. But he started off by pointing to the very vocal support for the Greek Cypriot regime in our own House of Commons. Does he not think that with a Labour Government in power here, the Greek Cypriots have, in fact, been emboldened to continue on their present course?

Q.   To use the House of Commons style, would the speaker not agree that it serves no useful purpose to speculate on what will happen if and when Turkey becomes a member of the European Union? We are talking about something which may, or may not, happen in ten years, or fifteen years, or perhaps twenty years' time, by when Europe will be different, Turkey will be different and Cyprus will be different, and certainly the demography, the demographic balance in Cyprus, will be totally different. An argument which is based on the proposition that since concessions would have to be made if and when Turkey becomes a member of the European Union, they should be entertained now, is not really a very practical argument.

A.   The point has been made that the UN is not impartial and imposes the precondition that the TRNC should not be recognised as a state. It is difficult not to agree with this view since the Turkish Cypriots were regarded as equal with the Greek Cypriots in every major respect when the Republic was founded in 1960. The Greek Cypriots have their own recognised state, but not so the Turkish Cypriots. For the UN to insist that the Turkish Cypriots should now accept this inequality of treatment for their state is to impose an onerous precondition on their participation in discussions that has no justification in history.

On the question of the influence of the Orthodox Church in the South, at a recent conference an informed Greek Cypriot participant claimed that the Church now had little power or influence by comparison with the major political parties.

Are national interests more important than regard for human rights? A concern for human rights is a dominant feature of the foreign policies of today's liberal and democratic states, so we are told. But in the 1960s the rights of the Turkish Cypriots seem to have counted for little against the interests of the powers, who were intent on preventing Makarios from encouraging the Soviet Union, and thereby posing a threat to the British bases, at a time when the Soviet Union was dangerously influential in wide areas of the Middle East.

The international community should now sit back, it is said I argued, and say to both sides in the dispute that it is really up to them to come to some agreement. But is this realistic, I am asked, now that we in Britain have a Labour government in power, a development that must encourage the Greek Cypriots?

Certainly it would not be at all easy to persuade the Greek Cypriots to meet with the other side to discuss the return of territory to the Greek Cypriots, and the return to, or compensation for, property abandoned by Greek Cypriots (and Turkish Cypriots) in 1974. The Greek Cypriots would have to withdraw their claim to sovereignty over the North, which is the latter's principal desideratum. In my view it would be more profitable for the UN Security Council, not to sit back, certainly, but to make every effort to bring about negotiations of this sort before venturing again into the quagmire of constitution making. Have the Greek Cypriots been emboldened by the election of a Labour Government in

Britain? Possibly so, but recent Conservative governments have also supported the Greek Cypriots.

Do the Greek Cypriots not want a solution of the Cyprus issue because they would have nothing to gain from it? The reverse, I believe, is true. The position worsens for them day by day. For Bülent Ecevit, and for many others, the present situation *is* the solution. The Turkish Cypriots have all they need, save for international recognition, which would vitalise their economy, but recognition may anyway come about slowly and piecemeal over the years.

To turn to the interesting issue of what happens to the North now if the South is admitted to the European Union, in the short term probably very little will change. The TRNC, whose economy is slowly improving, will continue to survive with Turkish economic assistance and military support. On the longer term prospects for the TRNC if Turkey should be admitted to the EU in some ten, fifteen or twenty years' time one speaker has already reminded us that over such a period of time the European Union, Turkey and Cyprus will all be very different and Turkey might not then even wish to join. If Turkey were then to become a member of the European Union, with the TRNC still unrecognised, the TRNC would indeed be in a difficult position, as would Turkey, but to take any steps now (if that is the heart of the question) to prepare for Turkey's possible, and only *possible*, membership of the EU at some distant date would seem premature.

Finally, I was asked to say whether I was optimistic. The growing recognition on the Greek side that the situation is at impasse is, paradoxically, encouraging. There are murmurs in the South of late that 'land for peace' may actually be the only realistic option. Anxieties in Athens about the importation of the S-300 missiles into Cyprus and the consequent danger of a war with Turkey are significant. It is also clear that Turkey is solidly behind the TRNC with no exploitable rift between them. The UN Security Council is still, unfortunately, seeking the establishment of a bi-communal federal state with a single sovereignty, a single citizenship and a single territory, the Greek Cypriot desiderata, and has given no encouragement to the Turkish-Cypriot proposal for a confederation made in August 1998. Yet overall I am optimistic, especially as the international community seems to be on the verge of understanding the Cyprus issue better and is faced with an impasse that may well force new appraisals of a situation looked at for too long through the same lenses.

| 7 |

Foreign Policy
and
Domestic Politics

Dr William Hale

This paper seeks to summarise some of the main features and principles of Turkish foreign policy, and to try to assess how and to what extent they have been shaped by domestic political forces. Unfortunately, this can only be a brief and very speculative account, since the processes of foreign policy formation are one of the least studied aspects of Turkey's modern history and its current politics. The result is, at best, a research agenda rather than a finished task. It begins by summarising some of the main principles of Turkish foreign policy, and identifying the chief decision makers. A short account of how domestic and foreign policies have interacted since the 1920s is followed by a discussion of the main issues in Turkey's current foreign relations, and the positions towards them adopted by public opinion, the main political parties, and other non-governmental actors.

Turkey's foreign policy: actors, interests and principles
As in other countries, Turkish foreign policy is determined by two sets of decision makers. The first category can be defined

as state actors, since they occupy positions of power within the executive arm of the state. This includes the President, the Prime Minister, and the Foreign Minister, together with the commanders of the armed forces (combined since 1961 in the National Security Council) plus the professional diplomats in the Ministry of Foreign Affairs. Non-state actors include the political parties and their representatives in parliament, public opinion (a concept which is admittedly difficult to pin down), the media, and interest or pressure groups. The relative importance of the two categories of actors will normally depend on the nature of the political regime at the time – whether tutelary-authoritarian or pluralistic – and the salience of the issue concerned in domestic policy debates.

In the Turkish case, state actors have normally seen foreign policy as primarily conditioned by the need to protect and promote accepted national interests. Non-state actors will often approach foreign policy questions on the same basis, though on some issues they may promote views reflecting sectional interests or concerns, or particular ideological positions. The perceived national interests are normally defined as, first, to preserve national security and the national territory, while avoiding wars, or commitments which might lead to the country's involvement in a war where national security or other defined national interests are not clearly at stake. The promotion of global peace, in so far as Turkey can help to achieve it, is a broader objective. Second is the need to advance the country's economic interests, by promoting its international trade, and economic development and modernisation, and third, in some cases, to protect those seen as 'ethnic kin' – either as fellow-Turks or, occasionally, as fellow-Muslims. The last is, however, the most problematic of the three principles, and will be briefly returned to later.

In seeking to achieve these objectives, Turkey has certain strengths and weaknesses of which its foreign policy makers must inevitably take account. On the positive side of the balance sheet, in both the cold war and post-cold war contexts it has a vital strategic situation at the crossroads between south-east Europe, the southern part of the former USSR. As a member of NATO, it has generally good relations with the Western powers, and its own military strength is sufficient to deter a conventional attack by anything other than a super-power. The NATO alliance also gives it deterrent security against a possible nuclear attack. In the economy, it has experienced generally high growth, and has a flourishing private industrial sector, which puts it in a globally competitive position in a number of markets. On the other hand, judged globally, Turkey is a medium-rank power. Though it can protect its own territory, its ability to project its military power beyond its own borders is limited to some special cases. Economically, it is quite heavily dependent on the main industrial states for the management of its international debts, and state finances have been poorly managed. Its governments have been highly unstable at various times (including the present) and other domestic conflicts – notably the Kurdish question and terrorist attacks by the PKK – have made national security more difficult to protect, besides affecting Turkey's relations with Western Europe.

Domestic politics and the evolution of policy, 1923-1990
It seems fairly safe to say that, until the 1960s, state actors were clearly dominant in foreign policy making in the Turkish Republic. This was naturally the case between 1923 and 1945 when, except for a few brief intervals, Turkey had a single-party tutelary regime. Although divergent views could sometimes be expressed in the press and parliament, debate was normally controlled, and the state elite enjoyed a virtual monopoly of decision making.[1] However, this was not the only explanation, since, so far as one can tell, there was relatively little dissent about the main lines of foreign policy. During the 1920s and 1930s Kemal Atatürk enjoyed a virtually unchallengeable national authority, and took a direct and crucial interest in shaping Turkey's foreign relations. His

foreign policies were effectively continued by İsmet İnönü, his successor as President between 1938 and 1950. Once the treaty of Lausanne had been signed in 1923, Ataturk's main aim was to preserve the security which had been won and, in the medium term, to restore relations with the former entente powers (notably Britain and France, but including also Greece). In this way, Turkey could take its place among the respected community of Western nations, and avoid the risk of wars from which it had suffered so tragically between 1912 and 1922.

Balanced policies between the Western powers and Soviet Russia, with which Turkey preserved good relations until the Nazi-Soviet Pact of 1939, were also part of this formula. By the mid-1930s, the threat from Italy, and later from Germany, was a primary concern of Turkish governments. Unfortunately, Turkey failed to persuade its Balkan neighbours to join in effective security arrangements, or to mobilise the League of Nations effectively against Italian aggression in Ethiopia.[2] When İnönü's government signed a treaty of alliance with Britain and France in October 1939, he apparently expected that Turkey would be fully able to carry out its commitments under it,[3] but the collapse of France forced him to revise this. For the remainder of World War II, he remained committed to *de facto* neutrality, in spite of strong pressure from both sides to join the war. In none of this is there any clear sign of strong internal dissent from Ataturk's or İnönü's policies, even among the policy-making élite.[4]

These conditions continued for many years after the war. In 1945-46 Turkey was directly threatened by the USSR, which had not only taken over eastern Europe, but also demanded the establishment of Soviet-controlled bases in the Turkish straits, and territorial concessions on Turkey's northeast frontier. Turkey was forced to abandon its pre-war neutrality: it built up its economic and military relations with the Western powers, becoming a member of the Council of Europe in 1949 and a full member of the NATO alliance in

1952. As a founder member of the United Nations, it sent the third biggest national contingent to join the UN forces in Korea in 1950. In spite of the defeat of İsmet İnönü's Republican People's Party in the 1950 elections, and the accession to power of Adnan Menderes's Democrat Party, there was no change in foreign policies. Now in opposition, İsmet İnönü criticised some of the Democrats' foreign policies on points of detail but not of general principle.[5]

This general consensus survived the overthrow of Menderes's government by the *coup d'état* of 27 May 1960, but began to crumble in the following decade. A principle cause of this was the Cyprus crisis of 1964, which brought Turkey into conflict with its Western allies, primarily the United States. Another factor was the thaw in the cold war signalised by the era of détente between the superpowers following the near-disaster of the Cuban missile crisis of 1962 (in which Turkey was indirectly involved) which gave states like Turkey more freedom of manoeuvre in their relations with the two blocs. Third, the liberalisation of the domestic political system meant the emergence of a vigorous left wing in Turkish politics, which attacked the alliance with the United States. Nonetheless, a public debate in 1966-68 concluded that Turkey would be far better off within the Western alliance, both in the context of the cold war conflict, and its regional disputes with Greece.[6] During the 1970s the two coalition governments led by Bülent Ecevit in 1974 and 1978-79 attempted to implement what was claimed to be a more 'multi-faceted' foreign policy. In practice this had relatively little effect on the overall direction of policies, though governments under both Ecevit and Süleyman Demirel did succeed in improving relations with the USSR, in response to shifts in Soviet policy.[7] During the first half of the 1980s – a period sometimes referred to as the 'second cold war' – Turkey moved back to a more definitely pro-Western position. This was partly the result of renewed tension in east-west relations following the Soviet invasion of Afghanistan in December 1979 and apparent immobility in the

Kremlin, and partly of the suppression of the Turkish left by the military regime of 1980-83 and its failure to re-emerge as an effective force in Turkish politics under the subsequent Motherland Party government of Turgut Özal.[8]

Turkey in the post-cold war era: foreign policy and political pluralism
Two important features distinguish Turkish foreign policy since 1990 from that of previous eras. First, the collapse of the bi-polar international system has reduced the risk of nuclear war, but has substantially increased the number and complexity of regional international conflicts and problems which foreign policy makers have to address. Second, public debate and dissent on foreign policy issues has become more salient, and the variety of perceived alternatives has increased, so that domestic political pressures and debates have become noticeably more important in foreign policy decision making. In effect, non-state actors have become more significant in policy formation. This has presented the foreign policy makers with the need to avoid inconsistencies between policies in different theatres, and to balance domestic political pressures with external realities.

Of course these changes should not be exaggerated. Writing at the beginning of the 1970s, Ferenç Vali concluded that, even after the shifts of the previous few years, public interest in Turkey in most foreign policy questions was still 'skin deep', although 'questions affecting national feeling or religious sentiment are more likely to arouse deeper interest' than other issues.[9] Similarly, a survey conducted by the Strateji-Mori polling organisation in 1997 found that only 23 per cent of respondents described themselves as 'interested' in foreign policy questions, while 57 per cent were 'not interested'. Not surprisingly, these proportions were more than reversed when the field of respondents was restricted to university graduates. Supporters of the Republican People's Party were also far more likely to express interest in foreign policy than those of other parties. In their manifestos issued for the general elections of December 1995,[10] none of the five main parties devoted more than about 5-6 per cent of their space to foreign policy questions. Predictably, domestic issues - notably economic and social policy, law and order and the fight against terrorism, the question of civil liberties, and cultural-cum-educational questions - seemed to be of far more importance to most of the electorate. Paradoxically, however, the experience of the last ten years suggests that foreign policy has in fact become the subject of greater domestic debate and dissent.

Putting the case briefly, it can be said that three of the main parties - that is, the Motherland Party (*ANAP*) led by Mesut Yılmaz, the True Path Party (*DYP*) under Tansu Çiller, and the Republican People's Party (*CHP*) led by Deniz Baykal, have broadly similar approaches to foreign policy, in that they are all pro-Western and all support Turkey's bid for eventual membership of the European Union. Among the other main parties, Bülent Ecevit's Democratic Left Party (*DSP*) devotes a good deal of attention to foreign policy questions, calling for a 'regionally-centred foreign policy depending on national interests'. The party puts considerable emphasis on the Cyprus question, and disputes over the Aegean with Greece, on which it tends to be uncompromising. While it strongly supports secularism, it is also more lukewarm towards the European Union than the other secularist parties, reflecting Ecevit's position while he was Prime Minister during the 1970s. In a press interview just after the present government took office in July 1997, Mr Ecevit maintained that a 'region-oriented foreign policy' did not mean that 'Turkey is ignoring countries other than ... its immediate neighbours', but created the impression that relations with the EU might be less central to his vision than in the case of the other secularist parties.[11]

The most radical set of alternatives was proposed by the then Welfare Party (*RP*) led by Necmettin Erbakan, and can be assumed to have been inherited by its successor, the

Virtue Party (*FP*) led by Recai Kutan. In the 1995 election campaign, *Refah* strongly opposed the project to gain full membership of the EU, which it characterised as a 'Christian Union', and instead called for a 'Union of Muslim Countries', though it did accept the need to remove barriers to trade with Europe.[12] These commitments were reflected by Mr Erbakan's policies while he was in office as Prime Minister between June 1996 and June 1997, in which he appeared to be attempting to launch something of a pan-Islamist project in Turkey's foreign policy which was clearly at variance with the pro-Western stance of his Foreign Minister and deputy premier, Tansu Çiller as well as being cold-shouldered by a substantial number of important Muslim countries.[13]

The broad division of views between the secularist parties on the one hand, and Welfare/Virtue on the other, are reflected in surveys of public opinion, and in the range of attitudes displayed in the mass media. Asked to rank a number of countries in order of favourability, the total of respondents to a Strateji-Mori poll in May 1996 put Japan at the top of the list, followed by a cluster of Turkey's NATO partners (the United States, Germany, the Netherlands, France and Britain). Muslim countries, notably Saudi Arabia and Iran, scored moderate to low ratings, with Russia and Greece at the bottom of the scale. However, when the field was restricted to Welfare supporters, Pakistan, Iran and Saudi Arabia came in fairly close behind Japan at the top of the list, with the main Western powers given a medium-to-low rating, and Russia and Greece again at the bottom. In the press, the main national dailies (such as *Hürriyet, Milliyet, Sabah, Cumhuriyet, Yeni Yüzyıl,* and *Radikal*) support a pro-secularist and pro-Western position. However, the mass circulation papers *Zaman* and *Türkiye* take a more pro-Islamist or nationalist (or pan-Turkist) stance while newspapers like *Milli Gazete* and *Yeni Safak* are clearly identified with political Islamism. Similarly, television stations, which reach a much wider audience than the national dailies, are predominantly pro-secularist, but currently one of the main national networks has a more pro-nationalist-cum-Islamist orientation. More broadly, all of the private national TV networks have played a major role in opening up a much wider circle of debate, in both domestic and foreign policies.[14]

Pressure groups and other civil society organisations have now become important in Turkish politics, though much further research is needed to show just how effective they are in the political arena. They include the two biggest business organisations, the Turkish Industrialists' and Businessmen's Association (*TÜSİAD*) and the Union of Chambers (*TTOBB*) besides the two main labour confederations, the Turkish Trades Union Confederation (*TÜRK-İŞ*) and the Reformist Trades Union Confederation (*DİSK*). Alongside these are a proliferating number of associations promoting women's rights, environmental protection, human rights and other public policy causes. Apart from the pro-Kurdish People's Democracy Party (*HADEP*) there are also societies representing specific ethnic groups, such as Bosnians, Chechens and others, though their role in foreign policy making needs investigation. In the absence of reliable information, it seems safe to say that the big majority of these support secular democracy, and the main business organisations are in favour of strengthening Turkey's links with the EU.[15] On the other hand, there are a number of Islamist civil society organisations, a pro-Islamist business group, the Independent Industrialists' and Businessmen's Association (*MÜSİAD*) and a related labour confederation (*MİSK*).

These points can be illustrated by referring to Turkish policies in the main theatres of foreign policy in recent years. On the crucial question of policies towards the EU, the main differences between the pro-secularist and Islamist parties have already been referred to. Over the last year, following the decision at the EU's Luxembourg summit of December 1997 to leave Turkey off the list of candidates for the next EU enlargement, Turkey's relations with Brussels have been going through a difficult period. During 1998, it appeared that the two sides might be moving back towards one another, but relations were then thrown badly off course by the dramatic arrest of the PKK terrorist leader Abdullah Öcalan at Rome airport on 12 November. There was an interesting and striking contrast in reactions on the two sides. While the affair provoked dissension, confusion and attempted buck-passing on the Italian side, and in the EU more generally, the (now receding) prospect that Öcalan might be granted political asylum in Italy, or would try to use his Italian refuge as a propaganda base, provoked almost universal ire among the Turks, and an unofficial consumer boycott of Italian goods. Among the main secularist parties, there seemed to be no clear sign that Turkey wished to abandon its European ambitions. However, Bülent Ecevit was probably reflecting a quite widespread popular reaction when, repeating his earlier line, he reminded the readers of the German magazine Stern that the Customs Union agreement of 1995 and the Annra Agreement of 1964 confirmed Turkey's eligibility for eventual EU membership. However, he added that 'Europe is very important for us, but the world is not solely composed of Europe. Besides being a European country, Turkey is also a Balkan, a Middle Eastern, and a Mediterranean country', besides having important relations with Russia and Central Asia. 'Hence, we are in a situation where we can open up to both east and west'.[16]

Of the other theatres in which Turkish foreign policy is engaged, it would probably be safe to say that relations with Greece and policy towards Cyprus probably encounter the least internal dissent: that is to say that virtually all parties and groups of opinion in Turkey agree that the government should act to protect the interests of the Turkish Cypriots, preferably by establishing a bi-communal federal or confederal structure on the island, though it is recognised that the Turkish Cypriot leadership has to play the major role in negotiating this. Similarly, Turkey should protect its interests in the Aegean, on the basis of the balance established by the Treaty of Lausanne.

There may be differences in the degree of salience which the different parties attach to these issues (for instance, the DSP devotes more attention to them than do the other main parties) but no fundamental divisions on points of principle. At the same time, it appears that relations with Greece have a less dominating position in the Turkish outlook than relations with Turkey have in Greece.

Turkish policy towards the other Balkan countries - in particular, the states of ex-Yugoslavia - is another field in which there have been strong domestic pressures, but which has generally been effectively handled by Turkish governments and diplomats. During the most critical phase of the Bosnian conflict, during 1992-95, there was strong public sympathy in Turkey for the Bosnian Muslims, in the face of Western inability or refusal to prevent massacres and ethnic cleansing by the Serbs. The fact that the Bosnian Muslims are not ethically Turkish appeared to be of less importance than their attachment to the Muslim faith, although the Bosnian-Muslim identity also has a strong element of secularism. Public campaigns on this issue were promoted by the then opposition parties - notably the Welfare Party, *ANAP*, the *DSP* and the ultranationalist Nationalist Movement Party (*MHP*), as well as President Turgut Özal, until his death in April 1993. These parties had a higher profile in public protests than organisations of Bosnian Muslims settled in Turkey.[17] On the other hand, the government clearly indicated that Turkey would be politically and militarily unable to intervene unilaterally, and that its most effective policy would be to press for international action through the UN, NATO, and other multilateral bodies. Hence, it played an active role in the UN Protection Force (UNPROFOR) and the present NATO implementation force in Bosnia-Herzegovina, besides accepting some 200,000 refugees from Bosnia. Diplomatically, its main role was to bring together the Bosnian Muslims and Croats, in which respect it is recognised to have played an effective part.[18] In this way, it managed to balance internal pressures and external realities skilfully, and keep the question as a humanitarian one, rather than a Huntingtonian 'clash of civilisations', Christian versus Muslim.

Turkey's policies towards another regional problem, that of the conflict between Armenia and Azerbaijan, are affected by quite similar considerations. On the one hand, the Azeris are seen in Turkey as fellow-Turks as well as fellow-Muslims, whereas there are strong historically based hostilities between the Armenians and Turkey. Calls for a closer involvement on the Azeri side are voiced by Islamist-nationalist circles. On the other hand, Turkey would gain nothing as a state by direct military involvement in the conflict, and also needs to preserve at least workable relations with Russia, as its main supplier of natural gas and an important export market, as well as a valuable field of activity for Turkish construction companies. Hence, Turkish governments have steered clear of giving any military guarantees to Azerbaijan, and have put the main emphasis on encouraging greater co-operation between all the Black Sea countries (which for these purposes include both Azerbaijan and Armenia) through such projects as the Black Sea Economic Co-operation zone, originally launched by Turgut Özal. Turkey operates a trade embargo against Armenia, and has failed to establish diplomatic relations with Yerevan, but has made it clear it would be happy to do so if the Armenians withdrew from occupied Azeri territory. It also supports and participates in the peace process under the Minsk group. In this respect, again, Turkish diplomacy has carried out quite a successful balancing act between domestic political pressures and external conditions and interests.[19]

Finally, Turkey's relations with the Middle Eastern states have emerged as an important focus of debate. Having previously stayed on the sidelines in Middle Eastern conflicts, Turkey was unexpectedly thrust into the front line by the Gulf crisis of 1990-91. Although there was never any serious doubt that Turkey would adhere to UN Security Council decisions by applying an economic embargo on Iraq and demanding Iraqi withdrawal from Kuwait, there was great reluctance to get dragged into a prospective war in which clear national interests could not be identified. In an interview on Turkish television in January 1991, President Özal admitted that he had wanted to send Turkish troops to join the coalition forces in the Gulf,[20] but he was evidently unable to achieve this, thanks to opposition within his own cabinet and parliament. An active engagement in the Gulf war was not only opposed by the opposition parties, but also a substantial group within Özal's own Motherland Party, led by the former Foreign Minister and later Prime Minister Mesut Yılmaz. In his memoirs, General Necip Torumtay, then the Chief of the General Staff, relates that President Özal wanted to open a second front in the north against Iraq, but that he never received any clear orders on this from the Government, and that he strongly opposed it. This was a major factor in Torumtay's resignation on 3 December 1990.[21] Hence Turkey's policy, which essentially consisted of reinforcing its troops along the Iraqi border, tying down about eight Iraqi divisions, and allowing the coalition powers to use the NATO airbase at İncirlik for air operations against Iraq, was a compromise between Özal's ambitious plans and domestic reluctance to support them.

Similar debates have been stirred up by Turkey's subsequent relations with the Middle East. There is little open public support for 'Operation Northern Watch' (formerly 'Provide Comfort') and when in opposition parties have frequently criticised it. However, when in office the same parties have recognised the realities of the need to prevent Saddam Hussein from re-occupying northern Iraq and to maintain broad adherence to Western policy: hence, they have invariably renewed the force's mandate (the U-turn made on this point by the Welfare Party after it came to office in June 1996 is a striking example). Wide divergences also appeared between the policies of the Welfare Party, in its attempt to build up some kind of international Turkish-led Muslim coalition, including Iran, which was strongly opposed by all the secularist parties.[22] As a result, most governments have adhered to the view that Turkey should try to develop friendly relations with both Israel and the main Arab states, while supporting the Arab-Israeli peace process and refusing to take sides in other regional conflicts. While this approach may be criticised by the Islamists, it appears to be supported by the bulk of public opinion.

Over the last three years, Turkey's rapprochement with Israel has also become a focus of debate among both Turkish and foreign observers. For some, the military cooperation agreement signed between the two countries in February 1996 is seen as a sign of the power of the Turkish military and the state establishment over populist Islamism.[23] Certainly, the question of relations with Israel appears to open a fairly wide division in Turkish public opinion, with determined secularists normally taking a more pro-Israeli position, and Islamists giving more support to the Arab side (though not to Syria in its bilateral contests with Turkey).

However, the position is more complex than this straightforward binary divide might suggest. In the first place, there is a strong pragmatic and non-ideological rationale for the Turkish-Israeli entente, based on the fact that a cooperative relationship with the powerful pro-Israeli lobby in Washington is of considerable general value to Turkey in its relations with the United States, and especially the US Congress. Islamist support for the Palestinians is more often rhetorical than real, and advanced primarily as part of the Islamists' domestic political agenda: it extends, particularly, to the radical Islamist Palestinian movement HAMAS, and tends to be critical of the PLO and the Arab-Israeli peace process in general. Moreover, Turkey's state policy aims to achieve a balance in its relations with the two sides. The agreement with Israel relates primarily to join military training exercises, and weapons procurement programmes: it is not a general military alliance between the two countries, in spite of expressed Arab concerns on this score. There is no suggestion that Israel would be willing to support Turkey on issues which are not seen as directly part of Israel's own national interests, or vice versa. As a sign of this, the Israeli government made it clear that it was neutral during the contest between Syria and Turkey which led to the expulsion of Abdullah Öcalan from Syria in October 1998. In visits to Israel and the Palestinian territories in 1998, Prime Minister Yılmaz visited both Israeli and Palestinian leaders and Turkey has made it clear that, if Yasser Arafat were to declare an independent Palestinian state in the spring of 1999, then Turkey would recognise it. In this, as in other theatres, Turkish policy appears to represent a reasonable marriage between state interests, pragmatism and domestic political forces.[24]

Questions from the floor:

Q.   Could you say a little bit more about Turkish public opinion, popular attitudes towards the EU? What about the rejection by the EU of Turkey? What about the agreement by the EU to accept accession talks on Cyprus?

A.   This is an obvious source of concern, but do the people who write the newspaper columns actually reflect public opinion, and to what extent do they create it? With regard to the EU, public opinion polls in Turkey suggest that the public is really quite pragmatic about this. That is to say, asked whether Turkey should aim for eventual membership to the European Union, a majority will say 'yes' and a minority will say 'no'. Asked whether Turkey is likely to achieve full membership of the European Union within, say, ten years or in the near future, most people will say 'no'. In other words, they realise the problems that are there. The reasons for this are quite mixed. Some people quite rightly say if Turkey was a full member of the European Union, this would strengthen us economically. It would help to strengthen the Turkish economy, though some of that may have been met by the Customs Union, though not all of it.

The second point they would make is they would like Turkey to be a full member of the European Union because this would help to cement secular democracy in Turkey and set it in concrete, make it much more difficult to go back on. This is quite a powerful consideration among people, on the left for instance, who traditionally were not necessarily very strongly in favour of the European Union.

Q.   Could you say something more about the apparently close alignment between the Turkish military and Israel, certainly in the perception of the other powers in the Middle East? Turkey is at present by no means holding a balance in the Arab-Israel question.

A.   Certainly the most crucial agreement between Turkey and Israel is the military collaboration agreement, and this brings benefits to both sides. It enables them to develop new weapons' systems and it allows the Israeli airforce practice training facilities. There are other benefits of a non-military kind in that it especially helps Turkey's relationship with the United States given that there is a strong pro-Israeli lobby in Washington. On the other hand, and I think there is a misconception about this in other parts of the Middle East, it is not a military alliance. There is no undertaking that Israel will assist Turkey on issues, which do not concern Israel, or vice versa. In Jerusalem I was asked by the Israeli Foreign Ministry to talk about this, and I said to them then, 'I would not expect the Turks to do things for you unless it also happens to be in their interests'. Similarly I do not imagine the Israelis would help the Turks unless they also saw that it was very much in their national interests to do so on that particular issue.

The second point is that Turkey has recognised the PLO for a long time. Mr Arafat has been to Ankara since the military co-operation agreement was signed. Mr Yılmaz went to both Israel and the occupied West Bank fairly recently and spoke to representatives of both the Israeli government and the

Palestinian authority. Turkey now operates a Consulate in east Jerusalem, which is, under Turkey's consideration and indeed Britain's consideration, not legitimately part of Israel. So the imagination in some parts of the Arab world that somehow Turkey is involved in some criminal alliance with Israel against the Arabs seems quite wrong.

Q.   Reverting to the question of the European Union, it seems that one of the problems affecting Turkey's image as a potential member, is an internal one, namely the continuing trouble with the Kurds. Is it possible to say whether those who want to promote Turkey's full membership will address themselves to this internal issue, namely that they will seek an early solution, however difficult that may be, of that question?

A.   They will have to seek a solution - it is certainly difficult anyway quite irrespective of Turkey's relationship with the European Union - because the struggle against the PKK has cost an enormous amount of money: it has cost about 30,000 peoples lives, a large number of people were removed from their homes, and so on. Whether the PKK is beaten militarily yet or not is dubious. There are claims on the part of the Turkish military that it is. But there have been so many claims in the past, which have turned out to be wrong, that one has to be a bit cynical about it, but this issue has to be addressed anyway, whether or not Turkey wants to become a member of the European Union.

| 8 |

Discussion

Introduced by Sir Michael Quinlan and Mr David Barchard

Sir Michael Quinlan (Chairman):
During the course of the day so far there has been a wide range of topics. Atatürk's legacy has been reviewed in two very stimulating talks. We have also discussed the social make-up of Turkey, and been reminded just how absurd is the caricature which still occasionally, I am ashamed to say, one hears in Britain as elsewhere in Western Europe, of Turkey as an elegant and articulate elite masking a vast and backward peasantry. There has been a very good and professional survey of Turkey's economy, where it has come from and where it is now. The process of policy formation and the pluralist background to that formation has also been presented. We have heard, of course, about Cyprus. There has not been much about what is perhaps the other of the major things which complicates Turkey's relationship with Europe, and that is the Kurdish question. It would be interesting to hear if others would like to say a little more about that. David Barchard will begin on this.

David Barchard:
Pursuant to this question, there are a number of points to be raised, one of which is the continuing importance of Atatürk,

which has been brought out very well by our speakers. It is important to understand that this is not a cult of the personality, but a living force relevant to the social, economic and cultural situation of millions of people in Turkey today. This is something not well understood in the Western world, where people tend to regard Atatürk as a 1930s dictator who outlived his time before World War II. The relevance of Atatürk to individual people in Turkey today cannot be stressed too much.

Related to that, however, is a second point. One of the reasons why Turkey and Europe are having difficulties integrating is that the administrative structure in Turkey is largely one inherited from the Ottoman Empire and reshaped in the 1930s to meet the needs primarily of an agrarian society. Many of its rules and ways of doing things, and the scale on which things are done is still very much as it was a generation or two ago. Once this time lag is corrected, and the political and administrative structure moves further away from that which was appropriate to the inward looking economy from 1932 to 1980, then many of Turkey's problems in integrating with Western Europe will perhaps fall into place relatively easily.

The third point is that of the Kurds in the conflict of ethnicities. Once you move east of Vienna, you get into an area where nation states are, by and large, not highly accepted, where people have a strong sense of their own culture, generally a strong feeling that they are entitled to a larger area and therefore irredentism is a powerful political force. In the case of Turkey the situation is very different. Turkey does not have territorial aspirations. It is the residual legatee of the Ottoman Empire, and content with its present borders. So there is a mismatch between Turkish nationalism and the states around this periphery most of whom have, at least to some extent, sentimental or territorial claims of which obviously the most striking can be seen in Cyprus. This is another factor in complicating Turkey's role in the twentieth century.

The very striking degree of social and economic progress achieved by the Republic is well illustrated by the fact that a few years back now there was a very great time lag in the arrival of fashions, ideas and things of that sort travelling from the West to Turkey. This has changed now and is an example of how the cultural, economic and social relationship between Turkey and the other countries of Europe is beginning to change very dramatically in Turkey's favour. But there has been a reference to the role of Turkey as a participating, contributing member of the European community of nations. The degree to which Turkey has already become this is perhaps not always sufficiently appreciated.

Q.   Why is it that, for example, almost everybody one talks to in this country, who has visited Turkey, comes back absolutely delighted with the welcome they have received? They are very enthusiastic about the country. But at the same time there is the phenomenon, which has been referred to, of politicians, apparently failing to know about Turkish history and failing to accept the Turkish point of view. How is it possible to bridge that gap?

It is something that Britain and Turkey have in common – both are very bad at public relations – and although it is good to hear that things may be improving, there is a very long way to go. All the very encouraging things we have heard about Turkey today are not going to be made visible either to the political elite or the public in this country. This is extremely difficult to do and it does require more effort than has been put into it up to now.

Q.   I would like to raise the dreaded Kurdish issue. It seems that one of Atatürk's great, I would say, geniuses was that he was a very pragmatic politician, and one of his great triumphs was to create a hyper-modern state out of the debris of an empire. But this was in the 1920s and 1930s. For better or for worse, modern European thinking in the last ten or fifteen years has seen a much greater emphasis on minority rights. This is the case whether one likes it or not. It can be seen in the framework of the convention of the Council of Europe and in the UN declarations in 1992. It now calls upon the state not to assimilate the minorities in this inclusive French model (which is what Atatürk did) but the reverse, to actually encourage minorities to develop their own culture.

A.   It seems to me that because of this, if Atatürk were alive today, he would have a much more enlightened view of the Kurds than some of the people who claim to be the guardians of his legacy. It is a problem which Turkey is going to have to face. It is not going to go away, not just for Turkey, but other countries in the neighbourhood, too. Greece, for example, has the same sort of inclusive denial of minorities and even France has problems in this regard. It is one of the things that have to be addressed.

Other points from the floor:

1.   On the relationship between Turkey and Europe, what is of great concern is the European Union (rather than Turkey) being honest with its principles. In the Treaty of Rome in Article 30, the exact wording is: *'The ideal of European unity is to unify the diversity of cultures within the European framework, and each country making a contribution to this ideal'*. There is, of course, the diversity of culture within the European framework, Hispanic culture, the Germanic culture, Anglo Saxon culture, Celtic culture, and so on. But Turkey is in a position to make a unique contribution to this European ideal, the reason being that Turkey is the only country, which can offer a secular Islamic culture into European identity, and therefore to the European ideal.

2.   That would probably resonate with many views that there is a special Turkish contribution, but it is nevertheless the

fact that there are still many within the European Union, who are all in favour of pluralism, but not too much of it.

3.   Why do the politicians think as they do? Having been a Member of Parliament and on the receiving end of lobbying from single interest pressure groups, I can safely say that of the 630 odd members of the United Kingdom parliament, probably only about 40 have any interest in Cyprus or Turkey at all. The rest have only a vague idea based perhaps on *Midnight Express* or whatever, of what Turkey is like or what Cyprus is all about. But the Greek Cypriots have realised something that the Turkish Cypriots have not until quite recently: that there is a propaganda war to be fought.

Their shock troops are the Greek Cypriots living in London, who are very numerous. Very large financial and other resources have been put behind what has become an effective propaganda war. So, one finds that when Cyprus is debated in the House of Commons, there are eight speakers from the Greek Cypriot side, who have all been teed up, briefed, organised, reminded by the Greek Cypriot lobby. There may be but one Turkish sympathiser or somebody, who understands the Turkish Cypriot cause, who will come into the Chamber and give it priority over all the other things he or she has to do.

It is the same in the United States congress, but thankfully the Turkish Cypriots have now woken up, and Turkey, too, has woken up to the fact that that the reason they are not winning the propaganda war is that they have not been fighting it.

Reverting to the issue of Turkey's relationship with the European Union, it would seem, having been an observer of the European Union for some time, that Turkey's failure to win acceptance has got little, if anything, to do with human rights issues, in general, or with policy towards the Kurds specifically. The European parliament has been known to 'pipe down' at the end of the day over the question of the Customs

Union with Turkey when it was made known that for larger geopolitical reasons a Customs Union was needed as a *pis aller* to offer the Turks.

It would seem to me that if Mustafa Kemal were alive today, being the pragmatist that he was, he would be looking for other objectives, more realistic objectives than complete union with the EU. The specific question is: has any thought been given in Turkish official circles, or for that matter, influential circles in Turkey to the possibility of EEA status, belonging to the European Economic Area? This would be a position of exactly the same as that enjoyed by Norway, which has complete access to the market, without any of the corresponding costs. It would seem that if Turkey was to abandon this unrealistic objective of complete membership of the EU, and adopt something more realistic such as EEA membership, it might be a very positive step to take.

4.   As far as Turkey's involvement in Cyprus is concerned, the first point is from 1963 to 1974, the Turkish Cypriot civil servants, who found themselves outside the joint government were paid by Turkey. In fact, each member of the Turkish community was paid £30 by Turkey in its role as a guarantor power. Food assistance was sent to Cyprus by Turkey and Turkey made sure that the Turkish community survived until 1974. Another important point is that after the *coup d'etat* carried out by mainland Greece, the then Turkish Prime Minister came to London and consulted with Harold Wilson and the Foreign Secretary, James Callaghan, for joint intervention. Britain decided not to go ahead with the joint intervention. That is why Turkey had to go it alone.

Turkey cannot be blamed for carrying out the intervention on her own because Britain failed to honour her Treaty agreements not just in 1974, but also back in 1964 when she recognised the Greek Cypriots as the legitimate government of Cyprus. Today, Britain, by supporting the Greek Cypriot application to the European Union, which is a unilateral application, is encouraging the Greek Cypriots to violate international treaties, while violating that international treaty herself.

5.   What about the Turkish minorities in Europe? One could be very optimistic because there is a huge Turkish minority in Europe today. The war that Turkey and these people have to win for themselves is the right to vote. If they can have dual citizenship that exists, for example, in Britain, the shape of things will change. It will be a gradual change but it will change. There are partitions within the Turks themselves but these are normal under democratic circumstances. Therefore the more civil societies they have the better organised they get. They will present the European Union, as they already are, with a bigger problem. So this is something that the European Union has to think about. The best thing that they can do, even beyond fighting for the Cyprus issue, is to get our citizens dual citizenship in places like Germany, especially, and also to make the conditions a bit easier in France.

6.   There is the issue about PR and Turkey's failure to address whole issues of lobbying. I am part of an organisation being established at the moment called the Turkish European Foundation, which is to foster closer relations between Turkey and the European Union at diplomatic and sub-diplomatic levels, this being a non-governmental organisation. One of our keen interests is to try and ensure that Turkey gets a fair hearing on the international stage. One of the sub-aims in order to try to achieve this would be to form a network of people ready to respond to matters broadcast or published in the press, initially in the UK, but eventually across Europe as it is a European Organisation.

It would, for example, encourage people to respond to issues raised about the Labour Party's dealings with the Greek Cypriots recently published in *The Sunday Times*. The complaint *The Sunday Times* had about this is that there was no response from the Turkish community in saying how appalled they are that the people they have voted for have this association with the Greek Cypriots. It is just that level of apathy, or lack of organisation, which is what we would like to tackle. It does not take very many people to respond. One of the things we would like to try and do (I keep saying 'like to' because we are very near a full launch) is actually to form a network of people.

People here, who may have comments, may well be interested and would be contacted in the future in any event. They may come across items in the press, or otherwise published, to which to offer a response. We would follow something along the lines of the Jewish organisations. If you have a programme about Arab affairs or about Israel, you always see that there is both a Jewish representative and an Arab representative for the debate. If there are four people on a committee discussing Greek Cypriot affairs, there is often only one person (who would be a Liberal) from the Turkish side. Part of this derives from not ensuring that before you agree to go on to any committee, or to any organisation where you are going to speak, that there is going to be some balance of representation. This needs some organisation. It does need to be tackled and it is part of what we would like to do. I do not want to make a propaganda bid here but I believe very strongly and very powerfully that Turkey has got a great case, but it is not being put and that does need to be tackled.

7.   As a broadcaster we constantly receive propaganda press releases from every single issue group that one can imagine, from animal activists to political groupings of every sort. I have to say that the Greek Cypriot lobby is probably the single most efficient, determined, coherent and well financed that we ever come across. Last Christmas every single journalist in our newsroom, about 260 people, some of whom have never expressed any interest in Turkey, Cyprus or

anything to do with that, received a Christmas card by name, and a Christmas card of the alleged occupied area!

8.   It seems that one of the problems that Turkey faces today is the continuing and possible growing strength of political Islam and the fact that this does seem to have polarised Turkish society considerably. It is surely one of the most important reasons why the military are very actively involved in Turkish politics now. In Europe there is often not very much understanding of this problem, simply because although there is some degree of Islamic fundamentalism in European countries, it is on such a small scale that it does not threaten the democratic regime in Europe. The fact that the military appears to have had to take a more active role in order to keep secularism going is rather depressing, and it is worrying whether one should attach more importance to secularism or more importance to a democracy. Perhaps there should be more looking into consciences on the part of people in the West, asking themselves whether they would be so worried about military intervention and so critical of military intervention in Turkey if in their own countries they had such a movement using democracy to come to power.

| 9 |

Afterword

Professor Norman Stone

There is something that journalists should say more in articles. Whereas in many countries foreigners spend a great deal of time criticising the natives and vice versa, this is not the case in Turkey at all. Everybody is very nice about the Turks and foreigners do not spend their time in a kind of foreign ghetto.

It is easy for those with foreign passports and a bit of foreign money to go to an exotic country with touches of backwardness and say, 'What fun!', especially when the food is very good and the landscape is interesting. This is an extremely easy trick. The interesting question is that Turkey is not now to be classed as a backward country. Urfa, for example, ten years ago was a dusty two-bed one-horse town. When one looks at Urfa today, it is still very obviously a Middle Eastern town, it is after all mainly an Arabic and Kurdish settlement, but it wears an air of some kind of prosperity. There is an obvious economic life.

If one takes the road to Mardin one can see that the effort of the Turkish state is getting some kind of return. In that part it is quiet: one does not see any troops or police around. It is all owing to something which could originally have been classed with the Etatist side of the Atatürk Republic such as the Gap Project. An enormous dam is built, there are pictures of sweet little peasant girls with scarves on, and one expects that one will then get more steel produce than the United States. The Gap Project could slightly be expected to have that sort of air. But when one goes to the top of Nemrut Dağı, the eighth wonder of the world, to see the sheer size of the water which has been dammed and is going to be used to irrigate a part of the world, which has probably not been properly irrigated since the days of Sargon or Syrus, it is obvious that it is going to make a terrific change to the place. Turkey cannot now be classed as a third world country. That period is now over. Inhabitants of Turkey can take a certain amount of confidence and be proud that they have done it.

The question now is where Turkey is going to go from here. It is very interesting to study a comparison of the country to which Turkey should be compared, and this is Russia. At first sight Russia and Turkey are miles and miles apart. When one looks deeper one finds extraordinary likenesses. Some of this obviously comes from the heritage of orthodoxy which seeped into Turkey and which is still very demonstrably there. The habits of Turkey, where politicians set up one party and then desert that party, and the smaller the party the more people it expels, reminds one very much of the sort of political narcissism which one can find very often in the orthodox world as well, in Greece, for example.

There are more interesting parallels to be drawn. In their initial programmes of 1922-1923 they start off with remarkable similarities. The USSR was actually physically set up just a few months before the Turkish Republic was proclaimed. In the back of beyond in Russia or Uzbekistan one will find a Lenin statue. Similarly in Turkey one finds Atatürk. It is curious as to what caused all these statues to be put up. The two set out also with the same sort of modernising project, including literacy. They had in common that they both had to deal with the Islamic world, which meant, in the case of the communists, eventually coming to terms with various *tarikat*s and Sufi mystics, who went on existing in the communist time very much under the surface but were still there.

They started out with a common attitude to modernisation: a large number of dams and parks of rest and culture. Now one can see the results. On the Internet the CIA statistics of Russia and Turkey show that the average age on death of a Russian male is 54, in Turkey 68. With women for some reason in Russia it is 71, in Turkey 72. GNP per head in Russia is now one third of that of Turkey. The Turkish economy by any measurable index of size has overtaken Sweden. Russia's foreign trade is still larger than Turkey's, as one would expect with all the oil, gold and timber. But the total turnover of Turkish foreign trade is now two thirds of that of Russia. It is expected by 2010 that Turkey's foreign trade will be greater than Russia's. That is quite a remarkable achievement for a country where in 1923, if one reads the wonderful memoirs of Şirin Devrim, one could not actually get a table made that had legs that did not wobble unless you went to a Greek or an Armenian. Now Turkey makes fax machines!

There are two further facts about this. The first is that the other day a Turkish tile factory was opened in Wales. This has not happened since the seventeeth century. The other point is that the Turkish air force is known to be pretty proficient and has been making good planes all these years. Now the pressure on it is such that it has to farm out the making of spare parts for F16s to Slovakia. This is a strong Turkey which can count as just as modern in the relative sort of way as the Ottoman Empire would have done in the later 16th century. In particular it is overtaking Russia so fast that those ideas of Turgut Özal in the early 1990s of a Turkish presence in Central Asia are not altogether misplaced. The idea of Turkish presence in Central Asia did look fantastical - that the Turks were taking on too much, that it was a great bout of nationalist insanity. But now it looks like it is going to be a reality. Turks know how to handle the business in those parts. They bribe with immense dignity and it would not be at all surprising to find that at some stage a sort of common Turkic market will be found there.

If one takes the trends from 1923 to the present and

extends them somewhat then the future looks very bright indeed. Any journalist in Turkey looking at the various problems should always bear this in mind. It is a pity that there is not actually a book in the English language which puts this sort of thing in black and white. The books that exist in English are often quite well written. People like Turkey, they are very interested in it but they tend to absorb all too easily a rather two-dimensional view of Turkey without appreciating quite what has been achieved after all the ups and downs, particularly since 1950 and the arrival of democratic politics.

Turkey's problems cannot be denied. It is a country in which the educated classes very often make no bones at all about criticising a great deal of what goes on. This has to be put in some sort of perspective. The educated classes very often depended on a state bureaucracy which had its modernising projects in the 1920s and 1930s and was remarkably successful at it. To make the population literate with a language like Turkish, and written in Arabic by a very tiny number of people, is phenomenal. However, the problem with all state enlightenments is that they get eaten by their grandchildren. Scotland is a very good case in point. Scotland produced the very first state modernising project. As a hypothetical example, the Edinburgh new town is built up, the canals formed, everything in the modern world from television to sociology is invented, economics along the way, and one then finds that a torrent of peasants are released who pour into Glasgow and pull the enlightenment down.

In his book *On the Holy Mountain* William del Rumple writes about orthodoxy and does not portray Turkey in a very good light. His good ancestor was a Scottish enlightenment character called the Master of Stair. He applied himself in Argyll to a digest of Roman law brought up to date for the purposes of the modernisation of Scotland. It required a formidable amount of knowledge of absolutely everything in sight. The wind howled, the servant made sour cocoa, the rats scampered around and into the middle of this comes a piper and a large Christmas pudding. He says: 'The McDonalds have asked the Campbells for sanctuary in Glenco.' That was William del Rumple's answer. There was an original twist to this in that the granddaughter of this man was Lucia di Lamemor. This is an example simply to say that the enlightenment state cannot carry its project through by debate and if it had been left to the methods of democracy as it was then understood, Turkey would have remained stuck where she was. What she has managed to do is to produce a successful enlightenment and then to face the problems.

The problems started coming thick and fast after 1950. They came particularly in the shape of the shanty towns round Izmir, Istanbul and Ankara. It is still a big problem. Enlightenments have this sort of effect. People arrive fresh from the village thinking the streets are paved with gold in a place like Izmir. The families stick together and help each other. They put up a house during the night and they are often not too bad. Turkish left-wingers look at the shanty towns and *gecekondus* and say 'Is this not a terrible blot on the face of civilisation?' No, it is not. If one looks at the equivalents in Moscow nowadays, they are not that bad. The death rate really tells that particular story. They pour into the shanty towns. Islam is what they very strictly believe in. Some of them become quite well off and some of the parents of students say, 'If my daughter does not wear a headscarf, she will be regarded by all her relatives as a prostitute'. Everyone has gone through this sort of period of European history. In France the battles were fought in 1890s, and in parts of Germany and Northern Ireland to this day there is a kind of religious conservatism.

A democracy sometimes produces things that one does not like. That is what has occurred to some extent in the successful modernisation of Turkey in the last seventy years. Some of the people who defend the Atatürk enlightenment state do not really very much like it. On the whole they are the people whom a lot of foreign journalists meet, with very good manners, very interesting people with a hypocritical attitude towards the Turkish state and what has happened to it, in particular, a critical attitude both towards the army and to the Islamic side. Some posters, which have been put up say, 'Our battle is with the gangs, the mafia in politics. Our battle is with terror, the PKK and our battle is with *karanlık* (darkness)', meaning that kind of backward Islam.

These are serious problems and are produced by the success of the Turkish state, not its failure. As far as the religious side is concerned, some degree of optimism can be allowed because it is quite likely that in ten years, with the growth of the country generally, Islam will lose that extreme 'shariah' approach to things and will produce what has been seen on the Islamic side even in the days of the Welfare Party, and that is some very sensible talking about the place of Islam in the modern world.

What is of concern is that people say the army should step in and stop extreme Islam. The army deserves much sympathy in this but the job should really be done by the political parties. Eighty per cent of Turks vote for parties which may to some extent sympathise with Islam but believe in the secularist state. The crippling weakness at the moment is that these politicians fight each other and it is very difficult to hit them on the head, as one would do with Italian politicians, and say: 'You must not go on like this because it is dangerous', and it means that the army will be put into a position, which armies should not really be in, not least for the sake of Turkey's public opinion and Turkey's effect on Europe.

As to the Turkish position in Europe the nature of the Turkish population in Germany is very worrying. It is a German problem, not a Dutch problem, certainly not a British problem. If one says one is Turkish in the UK it sounds slightly exotic but that is that. It is certainly not a French problem. But Germany is a problem. If one goes wandering through the back streets of Köln one sees the third generation of Turks. They have lost that natural style and self-composure that the Turks have, even in the back of beyond in places like Göreme. They have become German in the sense that they are loud and rowdy, they wear these absurd modern clothes and they have sown up the protection rackets. About 13,000 of a population of nearly 3 million go to university and it is a pretty dismal sight.

What is causing it is not clear but it took the Poles in the Ruhr four generations to become integrated. Germany is just that sort of place. In the fifth generation they become integrated into the Hamburg football team and the politbureau of the DDR. There is a fear that the Turkish minority in Germany, far from being a help, is going to be a great ball and chain giving Turkey a bad name, as to some extent has happened with Chancellor Kohl's otherwise desperately clumsy rejection of the Turkish claim to be part of the European Community.

As to the business of the appeal, there is one suggestion that can be made. Rather than asking to join Europe in its present state with its enormous agricultural subsidies, with its fantastically elaborate *acquis communautaire*, 80,000 pages of detailed issues about Telecoms and sardine tins and the wording of warnings on cigarette packets of unbelievable gobbledygook, there is one change that must be made and that is to get Turkish students in western universities on the same level as the natives. It is grotesque that Turkish students, who want to come to an English university, have to pay fees which are designed for rich Malaysians. It is terrible that this country can continue to do this. That is a case that could be sensibly argued. What Europe is going to find on its doorstep is a country of 100,000,000 people, which is growing at eight per cent per annum, a country which supplies a growing market for European goods and one which will become increasingly important in all sorts of ways. This country and Turkey are very well placed to co-operate and personally get along very well.

How Turkey stood up to the First World War to get to

the point of Kut el-Amara in May 1916 is an extraordinary mystery. General Townshend led his troops up the Euphrates, arrived at Kut and found himself cut off by floods and mud and surrounded by Turks led by Hilmi Pasha. After a time he surrendered with 10,000 men. In Anatolia at that time people were dying of malnutrition, disease and so on. A large number of these British prisoners died. Townshend's men were taken over and the officers went to officers' camps in Merzifon and Afyon. The men worked, as prisoners of war do, on the Taurus mountains part of the Berlin to Baghdad railway and many of them died.

Charles Brandon, a journalist for the Sunday Times, wrote a book in 1965 about that battle in (and it was the 1960s) the period of, *Oh, What a Lovely War* and one would expect a book like that to be written very much in the spirit of silly old fire-eating generals, brave men singing songs and general wickedness of establishments. No doubt that is what Brandon wanted to do. Then he spoke to 1960s' survivors of Kut el-Amara and there were sixty of them still alive that he could get in touch with. They all said that Townshend had been a very brave man and they actually cheered him as he went into captivity. But the interesting thing was that those sixty survivors all spent their summer holidays in Turkey with the families of the people who had looked after them on the Berlin to Baghdad railway. That was an extraordinary moment showing the closeness in misfortune that could come about. One hopes that that spirit survives.

Notes

Chapter 2

1. For an account of recent Turkish history, see Lewis, B. 1961 *The Emergence of Modern Turkey*, London: Royal Institute of International Affairs, Shaw, S. and Shaw, E. 1995 (1977) *History of the Ottoman Empire and Modern Turkey, Vol 2*, Cambridge: Cambridge University Press.

Chapter 5

1. Stirling, P. 1964 *Turkish Village*, London: Weidenfeld and Nicholson. For further information on Stirling's work see Shankland, D. 1999 'The Making of an Anthropologist: an Interview with Professor Stirling', special issue of the *Turkish Studies Association Bulletin*, Summer issue, in press.
2. Cf. Stirling's 'Introduction', in Stirling, P. (ed.), 1993 *Culture and Society, Change in Turkish Villages*, Huntingdon: The Eothen Press,
3. Stirling, P. 1974 'Cause, Knowledge and Change: Turkish Village Revisited' in Davis, J. (ed.) *Choice and Change: Essays in Honour of Lucy Mair*, London: Athlone Press, pp. 191-229.
4. On this point see my forthcoming, *Islam and Society in Turkey*, Huntingdon: The Eothen Press.
5. Sirman, N. 1988 'Peasants and Family Farms: the Position of Households in Cotton Production in a village of Western Turkey' PhD

thesis, University of London. Of course, not all communities may find modernisation so straightforward, and I do not wish to minimise the disruptive influence of social change. Cf. Shankland, D. 1994 'Social Change and Culture: Responses to Modernisation in an Alevi Village in Anatolia' in Hann (ed.),*When History Accelerates*, London: Athlone Press, pp. 238-54.

Chapter 6

1. Adjournment Debate, 28 October 1998.
2. Estimates are quoted in S.R. Sonyel 1991 *Settlers, Refugees in Cyprus*, London: Cyprus Turkish Association, pp.1-2. The total population reported in the 1881 census was 186,034, of whom 136,629 were Greek Orthodox in religion and 46,339 were Muslims. By 1960 the Turkish Cypriots constituted less than a fifth of the population
3. Robert Holland 1998 *Britain and the Revolt in Cyprus 1954-1959*, London: O.U.P., p.12.
4. According to Sonyel, *Settlers*, p. 17, a number of Turks left the island after Turkish participation in the First World War. By 1934 the Turkish Consul in Cyprus reported to the British Colonial Secretary that of 9,227 Turkish Cypriots who had opted for Turkish nationality only 2,000 had actually left the island. The British authorities sought to dissuade Turkish Cypriots from emigrating, seeing them as a counter weight to the Greek Cypriots, as reported in James A. McHenry 1987 *The Uneasy Partnership in Cyprus 1919-39*, New York/London: Garland Publishing Inc., p.161.
5. See McHenry, pp. 292-3, where this view of the inter-war period is shown to be prevalent in Greek Cypriot and other studies.
6. This information was supplied to me by the late Mrs N. Crawshaw, who was told about it by Sir John Barnes of the Foreign Office.
7. The fullest account of the politics at the UN which led to this decision is contained in the Introduction to M. Moran (ed.) 1997 *Rauf Denktash at the United Nations*, Huntingdon: The Eothen Press.

8. Earlier, in 1965, Britain, a Guarantor Power under the Treaty of Guarantee, declined to respond to Turkish demands for joint action under the Treaty to restore the state of affairs as established in 1960. When in that year the Turkish Cypriot deputies formally requested through the UN the right to return to their places in the House of Representatives they were informed that they could not do so unless they recognised certain changes in the Constitution, changes that would have abolished their status as equal partners in government as laid down in the 1960 Constitution.

9. Cyprus was an impediment for Turkey to good relations with Europe and the United States. The Turkish Foreign Minister is reported to have said at the time that 'Cyprus should continue to be independent, and that a unitary form of state could be adopted'. See Suha Bölükbaşı, 1988 *Turkish-American Relations and Cyprus,* Lanham/New York/ London: p.147, the source being given as *Dışişleri Bakanlığı* (Ministry of Foreign Affairs) *Belleteni* , 1969, No. 62, p.75.

10. Reported in *Briefing*, No.856, 30.9.1991. Bülent Ecevit thought the comment disgraceful.

11. See my 1998 *The Cyprus Imbroglio*, Huntingdon: The Eothen Press, pp. 181-92, for the texts of these joint declarations.

12. The announcement was made at a press conference at which the Turkish Foreign Minister, İsmail Cem, was present.

13. Security Council Resolutions 1250 and 1251 of 29 June 1999. Resolution 1251 contained the reference to the 'Government of Cyprus'.

14. For a brief introduction to these issues see my 'Impasse in Cyprus', *Briefing* No.1257, 30.8.1999. A fuller treatment is 'Confederation, Federation and Sovereignty: Theory and Practice' *Perceptions*, Vol. IV, No. 3 (September-November, 1999).

Chapter 7

1. The case has been examined in the case of policy-making during the Second World War: see, in particular, Edward Weisband 1973 *Turkish Foreign Policy, 1943-1945: Small State Diplomacy and Great Powers:*

Politics, Princeton: Princeton University Press, pp.33-71, and Selim Deringil 1989 *Turkish Foreign Policy during the Second World War: an 'Active' Neutrality*, Cambridge: Cambridge University Press, pp. 41-57.

2. The Balkan Pact of 1934 was designed to achieve the first objective, but it was structurally weak, and in the end none of the Balkan states except Yugoslavia were prepared to stand up to Hitler: see Mustafa Türkeş 1994 'The Balkan Pact and its Immediate Implications for the Balkan States, 1930-34', *Middle Eastern Studies*, Vol.30. On the second point, see Gordon Waterfield 1973 *Professional Diplomat: Sir Percy Loraine of Kirkharle Bt.*, 1880-1961, London; Murray, p. 221.

3. See Brock Milman 1995 Turkish Foreign and Strategic Policy, 1934-42', *Middle Eastern Studies*, Vol. 31.

4. For overall studies of Turkish foreign policy during the second world war, see Weisband, op. cit., Deringil, op. cit., and Türkkaya Ataöv 1965 *Turkish Foreign Policy, 1939-1945*, Ankara: Ankara University Political Science Faculty.

5. İnönü's Republican People's Party fully supported Turkey's accession to NATO in 1952 and (less enthusiastically) the Baghdad Pact of 1954. Later, however the RPP criticised Turkey attachment to the Eisenhower Doctrine of 1957, Turkey's support of American intervention in the Lebanon in 1958, and the co-operation agreement with the United States of March 1959: George S. Harris 1972 *Troubled Alliance, Turkish American Relations in Historical Perspective*, Washington DC: Hoover Institution, pp. 66-69. İnönü also criticised the Zurich and London agreements on Cyprus of 1959: Suha Bölükbaşı 1988 *Turkish-American Relations and Cyprus*, Lanham, Md: University Press of America, for White Burkett Miller Center of Public Affairs, University of Virginia, pp.35-36.

6. See Ferenç A.Vali 1971 *Bridge across the Bosporus: The Foreign Policy of Turkey* Baltimore and London: Johns Hopkins Press, pp. 158-63.

7. See Bülent Ecevit, 'Turkey's Security Policies' in Jonathan Alford (ed.) 1984 *Greece and Turkey: Adversity in Alliance*, London: Gower, for International Institute of Strategic Studies, and Alvin Z. Rubinstein,

1982 *Soviet Policy Toward Turkey Iran and Afghanistan: the Dynamics of Influence,* New York: Praeger, Ch. 1.

8. See William Hale, 'Turkey', in Yezid Sayigh and Avi Shlaim (eds), 1997 *The Cold War and the Middle East,* Oxford: Clarendon Press, pp. 267-68.

9. Vali, op. cit., p. 100.

10. That is, the Motherland Party (*ANAP*), the True Path Party (*DYP*), the Democratic Left Party (*DSP*), the Republican People's Party (*CHP*), and the Welfare Party (*RP*). I am very grateful to Aysegül Keçeciler for sending me copies of the manfistos of all the main parties.

11. DSP 1995 election manifesto, pp.98-96.

12. Interview in *Turkish Daily News,* 6 July 1997.

13. *Refah* 1995 election manifesto, pp. 6-7, 29.

14. See Philip Robins 1997 'Turkish Foreign Policy Under Erbakan', *Survival ,* Vol.39, pp. 82-100.

15. See, e.g., Asu Aksoy and Kevin Robins, 1997 'Peripheral Vision: Cultural Industries and Cultural Identities in Turkey', *Paragraph,* Vol. 20.

16. However, there have been differences in the past: see Mükerrem Hiç, *Turkey's Customs Union with the European Union: Economic and Political Perspectives* 1997 Ebenhausen: Stiftung Wissenschaft und Politik, pp.17-19.

17. Quoted, *Milliyet,* 8 December 1998.

18. Writer's observation at the meeting held in Taksim Square, Istanbul, in February 1993.

19. See Miomir Zuzul, 'Croatia and Turkey: Toward a Durable Peace in Southeastern Europe', 1998 *Perceptions* (Ankara quarterly) Vol.3 no.3.

20. For recent commentary, see Ercan Özer, 'BSEC and Regional Security', *Perceptions,* Vol.2 no.3, (1997): A. Suat Bilge 1997 'An Analysis of Turkish-Russian Relations', ibid, Vol.2 no.2: S. E. Cornell, 1998 'Turkey and the Conflict in Nogorno-Karabakh', *Middle Fastern Studies,* Vol.34: Suba Bölükbaşı, 1997 'Ankara's Baku-Centred Transcaucasia Policy: Has it Failed?', *Middle East Journal,* Vol.51:

William Hale, 'Turkey and Transcaucasia', in David Menashri, (ed.) 1998 *Central Asia Meets the Middle East,* London, Cass.

21. BBC, Summary of World Broadcasts, 22 January 1991.
22. Necip Torumtay, 1994 *Orgeneral Necip Torumtay'ın Anıları,* Istanbul, *Milliyet Yayınları,* pp. 115-16.
23. See Robins, op.cit.
24. See, for instance, the commentary by M.Hakan Yavuz, 1997 'Turkish-Israeli Relations through the Lens of the Turkish Identity Debate', *Journal of Palestine Studies,* Vol.27, pp. 22, 30-32.